Spinning Wheel's

Collectible Glass

Spinning Wheel's

Collectible Glass

edited by
Albert Christian Revi

Everybodys Press, Inc. Publishers

Printed in the United States of America

Introduction

It would be difficult to suggest one category of glass to a collector, for each has its own aura and appeal. Early American blown glass, while simple in design, has an elegance about it that some find irresistible. Victorian glass, colorful and gaily decorated, has its own special appeal. Art nouveau, art deco and contemporary glass are fascinating and a delight to the eye. And cut and engraved glass is fast becoming perhaps the most popular of collectible glass.

Since glass is such a popular collectible, the editor has chosen from hundreds of articles only those that would most appeal to today's collectors. The articles selected for this book are ranked among the most important contributions from glass experts in the last thirty years. In fact, material that first appeared in *Spinning Wheel* has formed a part of a number of authoritative books on glass.

Albert Christian Revi, Editor
Spinning Wheel
Hanover, Penna. 17331

Table of Contents

Early American Blown Glass

by L. G. VAN NOSTRAND

Stiegel Type

THE STUDY OF our early American blown glass is fascinating because of the opportunity it offers for historical research. In this, and following articles, we will endeavor to set forth a general plan for the study and classification of early American blown glass. This will be a condensed plan designed to give the student opportunity for more pleasure in augmenting the information by further study and research.

For the purpose of this study we shall classify our early blown glass in the following types:

1. *Stiegel Type*
2. *Three Section Mold Blown Glass*
3. *South Jersey Type*
4. *Mid-Western Type*

The glass made by John Frederick Amelung at New Bremen, a few miles from Fredericktown, Maryland, deserves mention because, after a few years of manufacturing, Amelung offered his plant for sale in 1795. During the period of operation he made many beautiful pieces of glass, particularly those which employed fine engraving as a means of decoration. Without doubt he made glass of Stiegel type and perhaps many examples which we classify as Stiegel were made by Amelung. However, this should make no difference to the collector as to the desirability or the value, since it is the *type* which is important.

As far as we know, Stiegel produced the first really fine glassware made in America. He did not create a distinctly new glass, but he did produce glass of fine quality at a time when quality glass, except as imports, was non-existent in the American colonies. There were glass houses operating earlier than that of Stiegel and they, too, could have produced fine glassware, but as there are no authentic examples existing, we eliminate them in this text.

Stiegel's workmen were European trained men from England and the Continent. They made the same type of glass and the same articles that they made in their native countries. This fact makes it practically impossible to state with any certainty whether or not the article was made in Bristol, Sweden, Switzerland or at Manheim. There are several pieces of glass in our collection which, in my opinion, were made in the Stiegel manufactory, but I cannot substantiate this opinion. I have never seen a piece of authentic Stiegel glass, although much must exist. But to prove a piece of glass genuine Stiegel is an impossible undertaking.

The scope of this treatise, starting with Stiegel, will extend through to the first half of the nineteenth century. Early blown glass of this period was made in New England, New Jersey, New York, Maryland, Pennsylvania, Ohio and some other localities. The principal colors emloyed were clear, aqua (color of window glass), various shades of blue, several shades of green, amethyst, and amber, running from light to dark olive amber, and some other colors. Some very interesting items of glass have been found in the vicinity of our early bottle manufactories. These consisted of bowls, pitchers, pans and other articles of free blown technique. The colors were aqua, amber, olive amber and, occasionally, blue and green. These items are rich in American history and offer the student ample opportunity for personal research. They would grace any collection and are quite high in price.

It has been said that the rarer the color the rarer the glass. This does not signify that green is rarer than blue or that blue is rarer than amethyst. If a glass manufactory has been making a certain item in green glass, then manufactures the same article in clear glass and of a limited quantity, then the clear would be the rare color and the value would be correspondingly higher.

How do we determine whether or not a piece of glass has been blown? Generally speaking, the answer would be by the rough pontil scar found on the base. However, this sign is not infallible. Certain items in pressed glass may bear this scar due to the fact that something external may have been applied, thus making the use of the pontil rod a necessity. As this text is specifically dedicated to our early American blown glass nothing will be written about our later Victorian blown glass. Some of this glass is very attractive and as valuable as its degree of rarity warrants. There are many collectible items found in Victorian glass. There is no doubt in my mind that some of our South Jersey type of glass is no older than that of the early Victorian. However, if it is true to type, it is collectible and of high value.

In discussing the various types of early American blown glass we now start with Stiegel. Stiegel made many articles of glass, some very beautiful and a great many quite common. According to his inventory he made cream pitchers (jugs), sugar bowls with and without covers, perfume bottles, decanters, tumblers of various size, wine glasses, beer glasses, Christmas tree lights, salts, and many other articles.

The common articles were made in clear glass. Salts, creamers and sugar bowls were usually made in shades of dark blue called either sapphire or cobalt. Occasionally a salt or cream jug would be found in emerald green. This would be the rare color and the value would be high.

Stiegel used various forms of decoration including etched, enameled, cut and gilded, various forms of the diamond motif formed by blowing the glass in a mold. The enameled ware it particularly attractive. This type was generally applied to tumblers and mugs, although these items were also made with the etched type of decoration, and others with no decoration. The colors employed in the enameling process were vivid and applied with old world skill. Castles, birds and flowers formed many of the designs.

Checking Stiegel's inventory we find that he made many ordinary wine glasses and these are believed to be typical of the early American blown wines that one occasionally finds in our antique shops. I am firmly convinced that in collecting these early blown wine glasses that one has a great chance of having a genuine piece of Stiegel glass in his collection.

In the illustration I have endeavored to show glass which would definitely be classified as Stiegel type. The large flip glass in the center (Picture #1) is 8½" high with a top diameter of 6¾". Diameter at the bottom is 4½". The decoration is strictly orthodox, showing the adaptation of the basket and tulip with other embellishment of design thought to have been used by Stiegel at Manheim. This flip might be one of the large tumblers referred to by Stiegel in his inventory. The small flip at the left is panelled and bears no other decoration. The flip at the right is also panelled but bears the additional decoration of an etched border. Both of these flip glasses could be classified as Stiegel type, but not in the definite manner of the large flip in the center. However we can't prove that any of the above ware were made at Manheim. Adaptations of the basket and tulip design are also found on beer mugs and spirits bottles.

In illustration #2, we show the same large flip as shown in illustration #1, along with a similar flip, but with a different type of etched decoration. The glass at the right and smaller flips of similar design have been designated as Stiegel type. I have very serious doubts as to the authenticity of this statement. I have seen other specimens of glass with similar design which have been definitely placed as of Pittsburgh manufacture. I think that this flip was made in the Pittsburgh area from 1835 to 1840. Even if not of Stiegel type, it is a fine specimen of early blown glass and should be a welcome addition to any collection.

A great many pieces of Stiegel type glass have the appearance of being slightly off balance. This is particularly true of the cream jugs. On comparing the two large flips shown in illustration #2, we find that the flip glass on the right has the greater diameter of base which give it a more stable appearance.

Shown in illustration No. 3 is a group of typical Stiegel type glass. Top Row. No. 1 is a blown salt of sapphire blue. No. 2 is a vertical ribbed pitcher of sapphire blue. No. 3 is a sapphire blue blown salt with ogee bowl.

Top Row. #1 is a blown salt of sapphire blue. #2 is a vertical ribbed pitcher of sapphire blue. #3 is a sapphire blue blown salt with ogee bowl.

Bottom Row. #1 is a sapphire blue creamer with expanded ogivals and has crimping under the handle. #2 is a rare sugar bowl with cover of expanded ogivals. The foot is small in diameter, which gives the traditional Stiegel appearance of being top heavy. The color is of a brilliant sapphire blue.

#3 is a Stiegel type creamer in cobalt blue and blown in the diamond latticed pattern. This creamer also has the appearance of being off balance and top heavy.

Illustration No. 4 shows a creamer and bowl of Stiegel type. The creamer is quite small in size, only three and a quarter inches high. The decoration is of the blown diamond motif. The handle is

beautiful and unique in design and application.

The bowl on the right is of small expanded diamonds and the body rests on a small circular foot. Height of the bowl is 1 7/8" and the diameter is 4". The color is of emerald green.

Illustration No. 5 shows two amethyst perfume bottles of Stiegel type. The bottle on the left is $4\frac{1}{2}$'' high and employs a pattern of expanded ogivals. The color is brilliant amethyst. The bottle at the right is $5\frac{3}{4}$'' high and the decoration is of small expanded ogivals. The glass is brilliant and the color is amethyst. These chestnut shaped bottles must not be confused with bottles of similar shape which were blown at a later date in the Pittsburgh-Ohio area. For comparison, the Pittsburgh-Ohio bottles will be described and illustrated in a later article.

Illustration #6 shows a vase of Amelung type. It has been classified as of Amelung manufacture due to the fact that practically the same engraving has been found on authentic Amelung glass. It was probably made in the Pittsburgh area in the first quarter of the nineteenth century.

The enameled beaker in Illustration #6 is considered a Stiegel type, on good authority. Stiegel's papers include records of at least four expert glass enamelers and decorators.

Three Section Mold Blown Glass

1

THREE SECTION mold blown glass, as the name implies, was blown in full sized three-section molds. The design was cut on the inside of the mold and the three sections were held in proper position by means of hinges or pins. These sectionalized molds allowed easy removal of the blown bubble without destroying the pattern.

It is of general opinion that this type of glass was the first to be manufactured in America with the idea of mass production on a limited scale, and was made to compete with expensive cut glass, English, Irish or domestic.

For the purpose of classification, the accepted designs used in the manufacture of three-section mold blown glass are as follows:

(a) Geometric
(b) Baroque (or shell)
(c) Arched (or Gothic)

The Geometric type of three section mold blown glass is made up of many patterns employing the use of vertical ribbing, bands of diamond diapering, oblique ribbing, herringbone motifs, horizontal ribbing, sunbursts, and spiral ribbing. These elements are assembled with geometric precision in forming the finished design. The most common type of pattern is the one where the full sized article of glass has been divided into three horizontal bands with the upper and lower bands having vertical ribbing and the central band having a simple motif of diamond diapering.

Illustration #2 shows a decanter of common geometric type using a central band of diamond diapering and having the upper and lower bands employing vertical ribbing. The blown stopper has the same motif of design. These decanters in clear glass, while not common are not yet rare, and can be purchased at the antique shows or through dealers.

The Geometric type of three section mold blown glass is the most attractive type in appearance and the most popular type with collectors. The colors used were clear, various shades of blue, emerald green (very rare), amethyst (very rare), light yellowish green, and different shades of olive amber of the type that was used in producing our early bottles. The bulk of this glass was blown in the clear color.

The articles manufactured in the geometric pattern include decanters, pitchers, footed sugar bowls with covers, footed bowls, bowls without feet, shallow dishes, bar bottles, vases, footed salts, inkwells, wine glasses, whiskey glasses, tumblers, castor bottles, an occasional chest-

nut shaped flask, and other articles, employing a semi-free blown technique.

Illustration #1 shows one of a pair of clear decanters blown in a rare geometric pattern having the central band composed of alternate rectangles of coarse diamond diapering and vertical ribbing. The ribbing at the top and bottom is also crude and coarse. The glass is brilliant and of a very good quality. One decanter of this pair has the word "Wine" blown on the shoulder and the other has the word "Gin" blown in the same position. These decanters are early and have been attributed to both Sandwich and Ireland.

Illustration #3 shows a clear decanter in the Baroque or Shell pattern which, once seen, can never be mistaken. Other articles using the shell motif should be characterized as of the Baroque type. Although this type of decanter is scarce, the price is rather low. The glass is heavy, has a brilliant quality, and the general appearance is very attractive. I have seen a few of these decanters in pale blue glass.

Illustration #4 shows a clear decanter in the arched type of three section mold blown glass. Its body is made up of nine panels, each panel having the arched motif. While this pattern is rare and seldom seen, it is not particularly popular with collectors.

We have now covered, in a brief manner, the three types of three section mold blown glass. The preceding and the following illustrations should enable the student definitely to place a piece of this type of blown glass in its proper classification.

Illustration #5 shows two toilet bottles blown with vertical ribbing of Geometric type. The bottle at the left is of a rare shade of powder blue and the bottle at the right is of a rich cobalt blue. The bottle at the right has a blown Tam O'Shanter stopper. These bottles are very attractive and although not rare, are collector's items. Another variation of design would be the same type of bottle with spiral Geometric ribbing. All of these bottles are attributed to Sandwich.

Illustration #6 portrays a very attractive barrel-shaped whiskey glass in Geometric pattern with a central band of diamond diapering. Above and below the diamond diapering is the conventional vertical

5

6

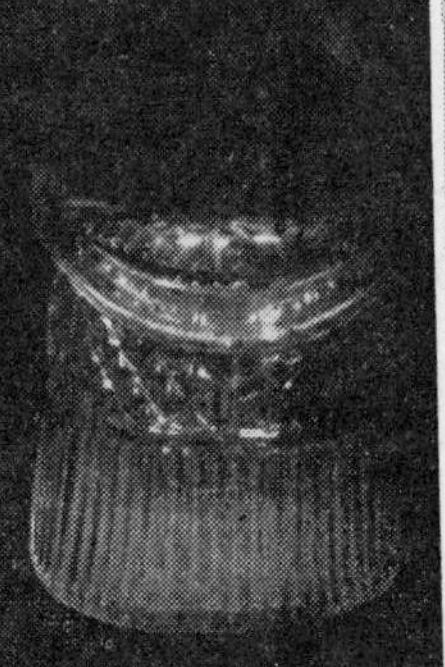

7

8

ribbing. Wine glasses were also blown in this same pattern. The color of the whiskey glass is clear and brilliant. A wine glass should be purchased for the same price. Flip glasses (really large tumblers) are frequently on the market and although not particularly rare are almost a "must" for a representative collection. They are generally found in the Geometric pattern.

Illustration #7 shows a three-section mold blown hat in Geometric design. The lower band is made up of vertical ribs. Above the vertical ribbing is a band of alternate squares of diamond diapering and common sunbursts. Above this band is the conventional vertical ribbing which has been stopped off to facilitate the forming of the rim top.

Illustration #8 is an attractive clear glass shallow dish blown in the Geometric tradition. The overall diameter is 6¼" and its depth is 1¼". The glass is very brilliant and clear. The design deviates from the common type inasmuch as the central band is composed of a herringbone-bull's eye motif while the outer band is blown in the diamond diaper design. The rim is folded under, which

9 10

gives it added strength. The dish is very desirable and would grace any collection. The prices of plates and dishes vary according to size and type of Geometric pattern.

Illustration #9 pictures a small clear pitcher blown in the common Geometric design, having a band of diamond diapering in the center with vertical ribbing above and below. The blown handle has been applied with great skill.

Illustration #10 shows a rare little bottle blown in the Geometric tradition. The bottom band is made up of the chevron motif. The central band is made up of vertical rectangles of sunbursts and diamond diapering, while the upper band is composed of vertical ribbing. This little bottle in clear brilliant glass is nine-sided and quite rare.

Illustration #11 portrays one of a pair of pint decanters attributed to the Marlboro Street Glass Works at Keene, New Hampshire. The central band of design is composed of alternate squares of diamond diapering and sunbursts. The color of the glass is dark olive amber, a color used extensively by our early bottle manufactories. These bottles are rare, although one occasionally can be purchased from dealers exhibiting at the antiques shows.

A mold parting line or "seam" can

11

12

be discerned at the right-hand side of the bottle illustrated. Examination of the piece also shows two other seams. These lines extend vertically from bottom to top without detracting from the general appearance. Other articles were blown in molds of two and four sections. For simplicity these are also classified in the three section mold blown category.

Illustration #12 shows the base of a decanter blown in the three section mold manner. You will notice that the rayed ribs extend inward to a circle and in the center of this circle is the rough pontil scar. All of the geometric type of glass shown in our illustrations bear this same characteristic. The Baroque and arched decanters have plain bases with the rough pontil scar.

Seam marks do not imply with a certainty that the article has been blown since pressed glass, in a great many instances, bear these same marks. Seam marks as well as mold imperfections were obliterated to a great extent by re-heating in an annealing oven. This procedure imparts a beautiful texture to the finished article.

A great amount of glass blown in a full sized section mold was made at Sandwich. A few patterns were blown at Keene, New Hampshire, some at Coventry, Connecticut, a few in Ohio, and I have seen several green decanters of Geometric type that were made at Vernon, New York.

South Jersey Type

WHEN WE SPEAK of the South Jersey type of blown glass, we indicate a type rather than a locality. It is not confined to the boundaries of New Jersey alone, as many rare and beautiful examples were blown in the bottle manufactories of New York State and the glass-making section of New England.

Often workmen were allowed the glass left in the pots at the end of the day and they made pitchers, bowls, pans, sugar bowls and other articles needed by the family. The color of the glass was the same as used by the factory and consisted of aqua (the color of window glass having a greenish hue), amber, olive amber, blue, and a combination of colors.

The artisan making these "off-hand" blown pieces could use his imagination and creative skill in fashioning the things that he wished to make. When you collect this type of glass, you are also collecting the individuality of the maker. If he had learned—and practiced—glassblowing in the Low Countries tradition, chances are his off-hand or "end-of-day" pieces were of South Jersey type.

The mode of decoration included the winding of glass threads around the neck or body of the piece, crimps on the foot, crimps under the handles of pitchers and sugar bowls, the lily pad superimposed decoration, striated (colored loops indigenous with the body), prunts (blobs of glass applied externally), decoration requiring tooling, and plain glass with no decoration.

The greatest amount of South Jersey glass was probably made between 1820 and 1850. Some non-certified pieces were blown prior to 1820 and I am convinced that some glass classified as being made at an early date was blown later than 1850. How late is early? That is the question which now confronts us. If the piece in doubt is "off-hand" blown, made from an early type of glass and shows the individuality of its maker, we will give it a passing mark and add it to the collection.

Illustration #1 shows a little tum-

bler at the left, a small pan with a folded rim in the center, and a rare small pitcher at the right. All are blown in aqua and all have the rough pontil scar on the bottom of the base. It is problematical whether we can place the little tumbler in the category of South Jersey glass, since tumblers of this type were blown at some of the bottle manufactories and sold as a side line. However, I have given it a passing mark and placed it in my cabinet. The little pan and pitcher would be classifified as off-hand blown and catalogued as of South Jersey type. All were found in New York State and it is very logical to assume they were made there.

Illustration #2 shows an off-hand blown pitcher with striated loopings

indigenous with the body. The applied base is of a dark sea-green, the handle is apple green, and the body aqua and semi-translucent white. This pitcher has been classified in an auction catalog as "Wistar", but it was probably made many years later. The two-ribbed solid handle has a particularly graceful flair and ends with a bold curl at the base. There has been a hesitancy in placing striated glass in the South Jersey tradition due to the fact that some glass of striated design was made at a later date and sold as a commercial product. However, as this pitcher shows individuality and fine workmanship, I will place it in the South Jersey tradition. Other colors were also employed in making these striated articles.

Illustration #3 shows a bowl blown in aqua colored glass. The diameter at the top is 10 inches and its height is 5 inches. The rim at the top has been folded under which gives the bowl added strength. The base has been pushed upward due to the pressure of the pontil rod. It was probably made in one of the early New York State bottle manufactories. Every collection of early American blown glass should, if possible, have one of these desirable bowls. They are quite rare, but obtainable from time to time.

Illustration #4 shows an off-hand blown vase in amber colored glass. It is 9 inches high and the diameter at the top is 5 inches. It is correctly proportioned and the workmanship is beyond criticism. I found it in a farm house in Wayne County, Pennsylvania. It had been brought in from Connecticut at an unknown date. The vase bears concrete evidence

of having been blown in one of our early bottle manufactories. The amber colored glass is the same that was used in making bottles and the top shows signs that the same tool used in forming the tops of bottles was used in shaping the top of the vase. I would place the probable place of manufacture as Connecticut.

Illustration #5 portrays two pitchers and a bottle. All are off-hand blown and executed with skill. The little pitcher at the left is cobalt blue. The handle is graceful and very neatly applied. It could have been made at any of the early bottle manufactories that used blue glass. The walls are quite thick which gives the pitcher a sturdy appearance. The pitcher in the center of the group is light amber in color and was probably blown in New York State. The color of the bottle at the right is cobalt blue.

Illustration #6 pictures an off-hand blown pitcher of a beautiful sea green color. It stands 5½" high and its greatest diameter is 5¼". The handle is solid and neatly applied. Fine threads of glass have been wound around the neck. The

center of the base has been pushed upward by the pressure of the pontil rod. The pontil scar is very large and rough. Pitchers of this type and of similar appearance have been attributed to the bottle manufactories of northeastern New York. This pitcher was, in all probability, blown at the plant of the Bethany Glass Works, Wayne County, Pennsylvania.

Illustration #7 shows a group of off-hand blown glass. The vase at the left is 7½ inches high. The color of the glass is very dark amber. The unique shape of the neck suggests it might have been blown with the idea of receiving a large ball stopper. It probably was made in Connecticut.

The pitcher in the center is amber colored. The workmanship is perfect and its appearance very attractive. The base is quite large and very expertly applied. Gadrooning has been tooled at the base of the handle. It was probably blown in the Bethany Glass Glass Works, Wayne County, Pennsylvania.

The rather large vase at the right was probably also made at the Bethany Glass Works. All of these pieces have very rough and large pontil scars on the bases.

Illustration #8 shows a group of off-hand blown glass. The chestnut-shaped flask at the left was probably blown in one of the early New York State bottle manufactories. The color is aqua and the spiral ribbing was evidently produced by twisting the bubble and not by blowing in a mold. It was found in a New York State farm house where it had housed the family supply of camphor for many years.

The large amber blown hat in the center has a wide and graceful brim with a folded under rim. These off-hand blown hats are very desirable, if blown in early bottle glass, but should not be confused with late blown hats of gift shop type.

The article at the right is a clear glass witch ball holder. If the color had been aqua, amber, green, or one of the colors of early bottle glass its value would have been very much higher. However, its appearance is decidedly in the South Jersey tradition, which makes it a very interesting little article.

Illustration #9 shows a blown footed bowl with superimposed lily pad decoration. It is the rarest example of off-hand blown glass illustrated in this text. I do not know the time of its manufacture but I assume that it was made in the 18th century. When held to the light, the color is dark smoky green and does not resemble the olive amber glass that was used in our 19th century bottle

factories. The glass contains a considerable amount of charcoal, particularly in the rim.

There is nothing difficult in the recognition of the so-called South Jersey type of glass. The term "South Jerey" is the name in glass nomenclature for the off-hand blown pieces made in our early glass manufactories.

Mid-Western Type

"MID-WESTERN type" is the term now generally, and correctly, used to designate the glasswares produced within the

Ohio, Western Virginia and Pennsylvania area of which Pittsburgh was the centre. It is technically, a geographic error to speak of "early West Virginia glass" because, when the glass here considered was produced, there was no state of West Virginia; it was the Western Part of the great and grand Old Dominion of Virginia. Advanced collectors all know the simple category of characteristics by which Mid-Western type glass is identified. All collectors can readily master these. Generally speaking the objects called sugar bowls are recognizable by the contour of the combined cover and bowl; it takes the general shape of a pear. Most of the covers are high, and, as one commentator has observed, allow for the continuous presence of a spoon in the contents, whether sugar or jam, honey, jelly or conserve. The decoration on the pieces are ribbing, swirling, and various diamond motifs, achieved by forming in a pattern mold before final shaping and finishing.

Glass production started in this region in the latter years of the 18th century. There are advertisements of record having to do with the establishment of glass houses in the Pittsburgh area which indicate also that a firm determination to make the glass industry a success in the region was prevalent. Glass workers from the East had already started to "Go West". Window glass was produced along with bottles and hollow wares for an ever increasing population of what were naively called "emmigrants" from the original 13 Seaboard states. Green, amber, some almost clear glass and some delightful shades of aquamarine are the characteristic tints.

It is now assumed that by 1825 the production was stabilized as to general form, quality standards, and philosophy of manufacture in all of the then operating glass houses. There were more of these than most collectors think, established in Virginia, Pennsylvania and Ohio. The glass, generally, was a brilliant metal, blown thin, and with great dexterity and finesse. After this first quarter milestone of the 19th century was passed, the Mid-Western glass makers developed gorgeous blue, purple and amethyst colors of great depth and clarity, and a brilliant yellow green that seems to have been, more or less, the product of Ohio glass houses.

Illustration 1 is from the Mrs. Frederick S. Fish Collection, sold at Parke-Bernet. It is off-hand blown and is attributed to the Monongahela district. It is sea-green in color and it may be the product of the Bethany Glass Works, Wayne County, Pennsylvania where my own excavations have unearthed fragments of seagreen colored glass. **Illustration 2** is of a pale purple creamer, expanded diamond motif, and a purple sugar bowl, blown with wide ribs.

There are sturdy, heavily ribbed decanters, bar-bottles, pitchers, sugars and other utility pieces which can still be found, along with an occasional sugar bowl, in clear, cobalt blue or amethyst which, while not rarities, are excellent examples of Mid-Western type glass that can be purchased without denting the budget too deeply.

Illustrations 3 and 4 are characteristic Mid-Western type covered sugar bowls. No. 3 is blown in broken swirl pattern and is clear glass. No. 4 is of light green glass, blown with expanded vertical ribbing.

Illustration 5 is a vertically ribbed amber covered sugar bowl attributed to Zanesville. **Illustration 6** is a ribbed amethyst creamer attributed to Pittsburgh. **Illustration 7** is an Ohio type pitcher in sapphire blue. **Illustration 8** is an amethyst covered bowl with wide vertical ribbing. **Illustration 9** is a footed open bowl of amethyst color with semi-flanged rim. **Illustration 10** is of a brilliant yellow-green, twist ribbed creamer of Zanesville. **Illustration 11** is a light green salt cellar. **Number 12** is a covered bowl showing vertical ribbing combined with broken swirl ribbing. It is of translucent glass, a sort of moonstone effect.

Illustration 13 is a light green bottle blown in a 3 section pattern forming mold. This is Mid-Western glass, but not Mid-Western type glass. Which is to say it is of a style blown in several Early Eastern glass factories and also in the Mid-West. It is light green. **Illustration 14** is indeed a rarity. Prior to the development of expert knowledge and experience in American glass collecting this was, prima facie, a "Stiegel" sugar bowl. It is tooled in the diamond quilted or latticed ogival pattern, of brilliant light green glass.

No matter how rare any item may be by repute there is always the chance of finding an example and at a most advantageous reasonable price. Any determined collector can say "I intend to have some examples of Mid-Western glass" and have results in a very short time.

Amberina Glass Patents

by ALBERT CHRISTIAN REVI

IN APSLEY PELLAT'S "Curiosities of Glassmaking" (London 1849) brief mention was accorded to a parti-colored red and green glass composed of homogenous stock. "Flint glass manufacturers," he wrote, "produce beautiful red from a mixture of copper and iron, and sometimes accidentally; for instance, when the ordinary metal mixed specially for light green medical bottles is nearly worked out, (meaning the metal is of almost the right consistency to be used), it will assume the complementary color — namely, a ruby red; so that the same bottle will be parti-colored red and green."

Such "accidents" occurred (and the

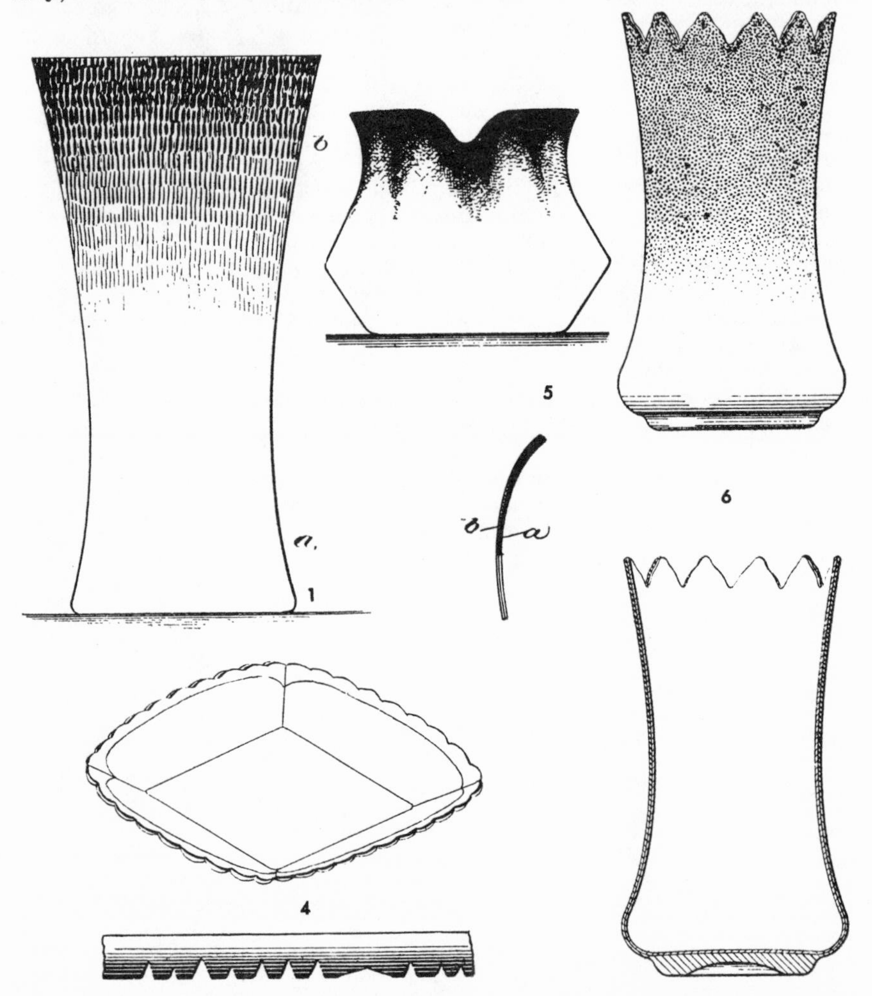

Fig. 1, *top left, sketch of champagne tumbler used to illustrate Joseph Locke's Amberina patent papers, July 24, 1883.* Fig. 4, *lower left, line drawing and sectional sketch of a dish used to clarify and illustrate Edward Drummond Libbey's patent papers for producing blanks for cut Amberina.* Fig. 5, *right, full and cross-section drawings of a vase illustrating Edward D. Libbey's patent papers for plated Amberina, dated June 15, 1886.* Fig. 6, *center, full and cross-section sketch of a small vase illustrated in Joseph Locke's patent papers dated July 13, 1886.*

metal would strike red in the reheating) most often during the "fire polishing" process when mold marks were being removed from mold blown bottles by reheating. The pieces to which this happened were considered undesirable and ended up on the cullet heap.

Many glasshouse workers in England and America must have witnessed this phenomenon at some time or other, but it was not until 1883 that Joseph Locke recognized the commercial aspects of this occupational nuisance and applied it to the development of Amberina. Joseph Locke had received his induction to glassmaking in the Stourbridge Glass district in England, but in 1883, when his Amberina was patented, he was employed as head designer by Edward D. Libbey, proprietor of the New England Glass Company in Cambridge, Massachusetts.

The patent for Amberina was dated July 24, 1883, and was granted to Joseph Locke, "Assignor to W. L. Libbey, of Newton, and Edward D. Libbey, of Boston, Massachusetts." It was the first patented method for producing shaded and parti-colored glassware from a sensitive, homogeneous metal. A very small amount of gold in solution was collodially dispersed in a transparent uranium-amber glass batch. Articles formed from this melt were allowed to cool below a glowing red heat then specified parts were reheated at the glory-hole. This rapid cooling and reheating struck a red color in the reheated portions, causing in the finished product a shading of amber to ruby red. The patent also provided for the development of a violet shade, greenish, bluish, and other tints though the controlled use of the caloric available to the glass worker by reheating articles through the small aperture of the "glory-hole" or the larger aperture of the "castor-hole."

This first patent for Amberina was followed by a series of similar patents issued either to Locke or to Edward D. Libbey. The next to appear was dated November 13, 1883 and covered Mr. Locke's method for producing a lamp-globe of two different colors from the same homogeneous stock. It called for the globe to be formed from a sensitive amber glass, and cooling and heating the globe unequally to develop darker colors where desired.

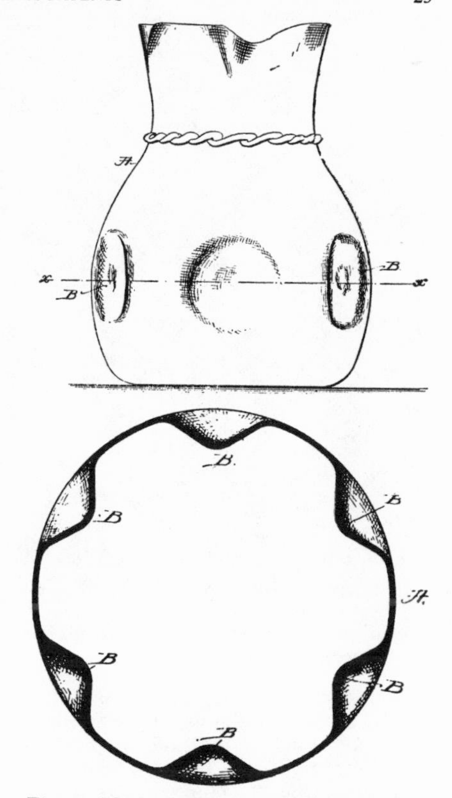

Fig. 2, *Glass globe and cross-section from Joseph Locke patent papers of August* 21 *and November* 13, 1883.

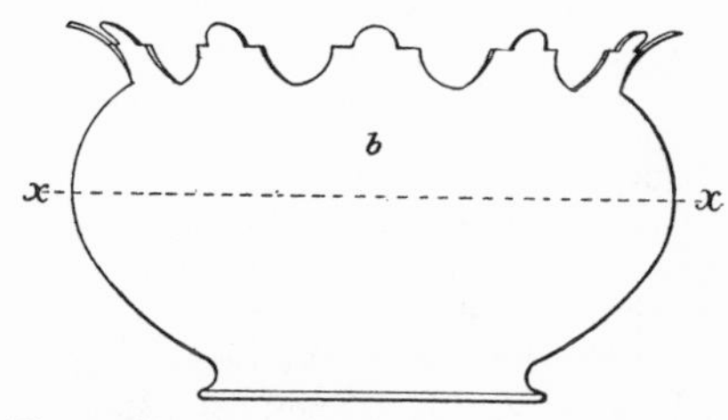

Fig. 3, *Line drawing of glass globe from Joseph Locke's re-issued patent papers dated February* 5, 1884.

Prior to this date, Joseph Locke had patented a machine for shaping or ornamenting convexed or spherical surfaces of glassware which simultaneously indented the surface of the article at predetermined points. Mr. Locke used the same drawing to illustrate this patent as he did for the lamp globe patent (see Fig. 2). Shaded portions are represented with darker tones at the top and around the middle at the push-in's.

Fig. 7, ***rare Amberina bowl with applied crystal rim, feet and decoration of flowers and leaves. Author's collection.***

Later, on February 5, 1884, another model of glass globe was used to illustrate Mr. Locke's method for producing lamp-globes of two different colors (see Fig. 3). Since this was a reiteration of his previous patent, it was classified as a "re-issued patent." It is significant only that Locke is referred to as "Assignor to W. L. Libbey, dec'd., S. C. Libbey administratrix, and E. D. Libbey." Obviously at the time of this re-issue, Mr. W. L. Libbey's estate was still unsettled. In all subsequent patents issued to Joseph Locke while in the employ of Edward D. Libbey, he is referred to as "Assignor to Edward D. Libbey."

In an era of extravagant cut glass it is not surprising to find the New England Glass Company also manufacturing cut Amberina. An interesting method of producing "blanks" composed of sensitive Amberina glass was patented by Edward Libbey, July 29, 1884. Fig. 4 shows the line drawings which accompanied his patent papers. The blank (in this case a shallow dish), after being suitably shaped in a mold, was reheated to produce a rather deep ruby color on its outer surface, considerably darker in color than the inner surface. A superb example of this technique exists in the Edward Drummond Libbey collection on permanent exhibition at the Toledo Museum of Art (see Fig. 8).

A patent issued to Edward D. Libbey, on June 15, 1886, for a plated glassware clearly explains the method used by the New England Glass Works to produce their "Plated Amberina." Hereby a piece of opal or opalescent glass, plated with a gold-ruby mixture, was reheated to develop a deeper color at portions which would blend into the lighter part of the glass, not sufficiently reheated to develop any color. When sensitive uranium-amber and gold-ruby metal were used, the result would be in the amberina shadings; a sensitive cobalt and ruby-glass mixture would produce a plated ware shading from pale blue to ruby. The patent papers further stated that colored casings of canary, blue, or green could be substituted effectively for the opalescent casing (see Fig. 5). While there is no mention of pattern molding to produce the ribbed effect on the surface of the glass, this had no particular bearing on the specifications necessary for this patent.

The last in this series of similar patented methods for producing shaded glasswares was issued to Joseph Locke on July 13, 1886. This provided for a glassware whose inner and outer surfaces shaded white to ruby (see Fig. 6), accomplished by plating a sensitive opal glass with a sensitive transparent white metal, and reheating in certain portions.

The name "Amberina" was, according to the application for trade-mark papers dated April 4th, 1884, in continuous use by W. L. Libbey & Son since December 1882. (There seems a slight discrepancy here, since Mr. Locke, the inventor of Amberina, did not come to America until sometime in 1883). The trade mark papers were issued to Edward D. Libbey on July 29, 1884, and the trade mark label has been found on specimens of plated, as well as the homogeneous variety of Amberina.

The Mt. Washington Glass Company of New Bedford, Massachusetts, also produced a shaded ware in every way similar to Locke's Amberina. Their glassware with colors shading into each other was manufactured under the trade-name "Rose-Amber." While trade mark papers were granted to Frederick S. Shirley of the Mt. Washington Glass Company on May 25, 1886, for "Rose-Amber," and Mr. Shirley stated the name had been in continuous use by the Mt. Washington Glass Company since August 1, 1884, no patent papers for this ware are on file in the patent offices in Washington, D. C. either in the name of the Mt. Washington Glass Company or any of the men connected with the firm at that time.

Fig. 8, ***Amberina mug cut in the "Russian Pattern", attributed to the New England Glass Company, circa*** **1885.** ***From Curtis-Libbey collection, Toledo Museum of Art.***

Mother-of-Pearl Glass

Left to right: Ormolu-mounted deep yellow Mother-of-Pearl rose jar with Chinese red cameo relief designs in flowers and leaves. Rare deep purple Mother-of-Pearl ewer-vase with applied purple handle and gold decoration of fern fronds. Sapphire blue ewer-vase with applied crystal threading, left in its original glossy finish.

by ALBERT CHRISTIAN REVI

Left: Turquoise blue Mother-of-Pearl vase with opaque-white cameo relief design. **Right:** Emerald green Mother-of-Pearl vase with Silver Deposit decoration.

FOR many years Mother-of-Pearl Glass, sometimes called Pearlware, has proved one of the most popular collectibles offered to a glass conscious public. The innumerable patterns in which this ware can be found, plus the many shades and combinations of color which may be encountered, make it to many collectors the most interesting of all the glasses fabricated in the 19th century.

The earliest use of a symmetrical, or controlled pattern of air-traps in a glass body as a decorative feature, the basic principle of Mother-of-Pearl Glass, was made manifest in the Venetian's intricate Vitro di Trina. The air-traps were formed by the criss-crossing of opaque-white glass threads between two walls of glass.

Benjamin Richardson, who was considered the father of the English flint glass industry in his day, took out what we believe to be the earliest patented process descriptive of Mother-of-Pearl Glass in the 19th century. His invention for "An Improvement in the Manufacture of Articles in Glass, so as to Produce Peculiar Ornamental Effects", was filed July 27th, 1857 and "Sealed" January 26th, 1858. The process for manufacturing this peculiar ornamental effect in a glass body was quite simple. A gather of glass was blown into a mold which carried the pattern in projected form. The result was a piece with surface indentations. The parison (the piece in its still molten state) thus indented, was dipped in fluid metal to coat the exterior surface. The air-traps preserved between the indented molding and the glass skin provided the ornamentation. Another method for achieving this result was to place the molded piece in a cup of glass blown to receive it, the worker blowing and shaping the mass further into the article desired. The several layers in each case could be the same color or of different colors, according to the desired effect the worker wished to obtain. Nowhere in Mr. Richardson's patent papers did he allude to giving the article a lusterless finish either with acids or sandblasting, as is usually found in the later Mother-of-Pearl.

Another method used in England and America late in the 19th century to produce this type of ornamentation

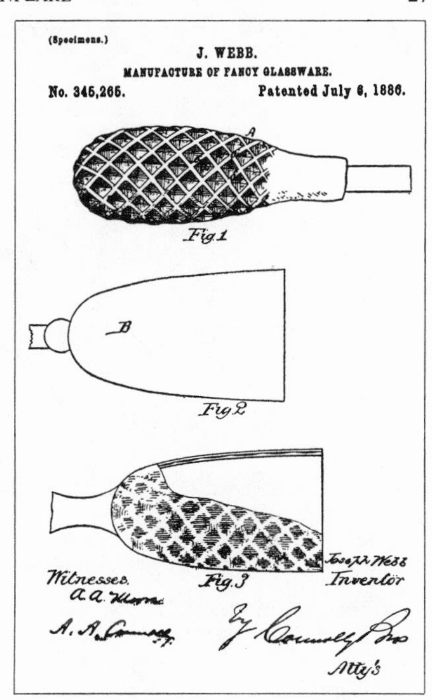

Joseph Webb's patent illustration dated July 6, 1886 shows indented parison, glass cup to receive it and cross section of finished piece.

was to line a heated mold with glass tubes, either crystal or colored, and blow into this mold an inflated gather of glass. The hollow tubes adhered to the surface of the blow and the parison was rolled on the marver (a polished iron or marble slab) to firmly embed the tubes of glass into the surface of the mass. By deftly twisting the parison while it was still in a plastic state the worker produced articles of glass with pearly swirled stripes on the outer surface.

On February 8th, 1881, a patent was issued jointly to William B. Dean and Alphonse Peltier, both residents of Brooklyn, New York, for the manufacture of glass articles utilizing a controlled pattern of air-traps within the walls of a glass body as a means of ornamentation. Messrs. Dean & Peltier's method for producing such a ware followed almost verbatim the principles set forth by Benjamin Richardson some twenty-three years earlier in England. No mention was made in the Dean-Peltier patent specifications to suggest a lusterless finish on the surface of the glass.

Large Mother-of-Pearl basket 10x10", with applied crystal handle and feet, glossy surface; pair rainbow-striped miniature lamps in Mother-of-Pearl with glossy finish, 8½" tall, applied crystal feet and decor.

Recorded in the English Patent Offices in London are the specifications for somewhat similar ornamentation filed by Alfred Landier and Charles Houdaille, both of Paris, France. Messrs. Landier and Houdaille's papers are dated September 21st, 1885. The specifications state that the decorative effect of the pattern-molded body, covered with a skin of glass to close in the air-traps, would be analogous to that produced by cutting or engraving. Again no mention was made of finishing the article with a lusterless surface.

Letters patent were issued to Frederick S. Shirley of the Mt. Washington Glass Company, New Bedford, Massachusetts, June 29th, 1886 in which he related his method for producing shaded and bi-colored articles of glass in cased glass, satin glass and pearlware. The process Frederick Shirley used to manufacture Mother-of-Pearl glass was the same one so clearly set forth by Benjamin Richardson in his patent dated 1858 with but two exceptions. First, Shirley suggested that the pattern-molded body be covered with a sensitive metal, one that could be developed into different colors and shades of color by reheating certain portions of the article in a furnace. ("Amberina Patents," *Spinning Wheel* March 1957 describes this shading by re-heating process.) Second, he suggested that the article be finished with a lusterless surface either with the aid of an acid-roughing dip or by sandblasting, all calculated to give the article a "velvet-like finish or an appearance resembling the skin of a peach", and "a pearl-like appearance."

It is significant that Mr. Shirley took out trade mark papers for a paper label on which the words "Peach Skin" appeared surrounded with certain hieroglyphics resembling Chinese characters. The papers also included another label on which the words "Peach Blow" appeared along with similar hieroglyphic characters. The trade mark papers are dated June 20th, 1886. The name "Peach Skin" might very well have been considered for Shirley's Mother-of-Pearl and satin glass although to date no such articles bearing this label have been found to support this premise.

Joseph Webb of Beaver, Pennsylvania, also patented a process for fabricating Mother-of-Pearl as of July 6th, 1886. Mr. Webb's method followed the cupping process explained by Benjamin Richardson almost thirty years earlier. In a subsequent patent issued to Joseph Webb May 17th, 1887 the manufacturing process did not differ perceptively from his first patent. Still a third patent was issued to Mr. Webb, March 6th, 1888 in which he prescribed the use of two molds: one to pattern the inner wall or shell of the article, the other to be used after the outer shell of metal had been applied. The finished product displayed a crisscrossed network of indented lines in the surface of the article.

In 1889, Messrs. Thos. Webb & Sons, of England, patented a process for manufacturing cameo relief designs on articles of Mother-of-Pearl. After the body of the article had been prepared in the usual way an additional plating of opaque-white or colored glass was applied to it. A design was painted on the surface of this additional plating with acid-resisting inks and the article subjected to an acid bath. The acid bath dissolved away all the opaque-white or colored casing not protected with the resist leaving a design in shallow relief on the surface of the article. A great deal of care was exercised at this stage of the work for if the article were allowed to remain too long in the acid bath the action of the acid would have laid open some of the air-traps.

Other English glasshouses manufactured Mother-of-Pearl. Stevens & Williams of Brierley Hill sold it under the name "Verre de Soir" as early as 1886 according to Mr. H. S. Williams-Thomas, Director of Stevens & Williams. A vase produced by a method described earlier, the one in which tubes of glass were utilized, is in the private collection of Frederick Carder, of Corning, New York. Mr. Carder told us, during one of our interviews with him, that he had made the vase at Stevens & Williams. He described it as "Verre de Soir with air-traps."

Signed Stevens & Williams, Webb, and on rare occasions, Richardson pieces have found their way into numerous collections in America. It will not surprise many collectors to learn that much of the satin glass and Mother-of-Pearl glass produced in the late 19th century emanated from Bohemian and French factories; some pieces have been found bearing the Sevres mark usually identified with porcelains of the period.

Glass manufacturers used many different means to color articles of Mother-of-Pearl. Mr. Shirley suggested that heat-sensitive metals be used for the outer skin of the article. By simply reheating a portion of the article different colors and combinations of color were brought about. An interesting process called "die-away" by the glass trade was also used to produce shaded glassware. The rainbow colored specimens so dear to many collectors were produced by simply laying what are termed "bull colored" rods of glass on the body of the article before it was fully formed. On Some pieces mica flecks and bits of variegated colored glass were picked up on the gather and made an integral part of the decoration. The decorating possibilities for this particular type of glassware were vast and in an era of over-embellishment every known technique was employed by art glass manufacturers.

Some other ornamental features used to decorate Mother-of-Pearl glassware were: silver deposit; colorful enamels, silver and gold leaf; Coralene and applied glass decorations of leaves and flowers, etc. Silver, gold, ormolu and pewter mountings have also graced specimens of 19th century Mother-of-Pearl glassware.

Extremely rare Mother-of-Pearl jardiniere with ormolu standard and a garniture set of apple-green vases with enameled decoration. The center vase shades from apricot to pink and has been decorated with applied handles and silver and gold leaf decoration of birds and flowers.

E. Varnish & Company's Silvered Glass

by ALBERT CHRISTIAN REVI

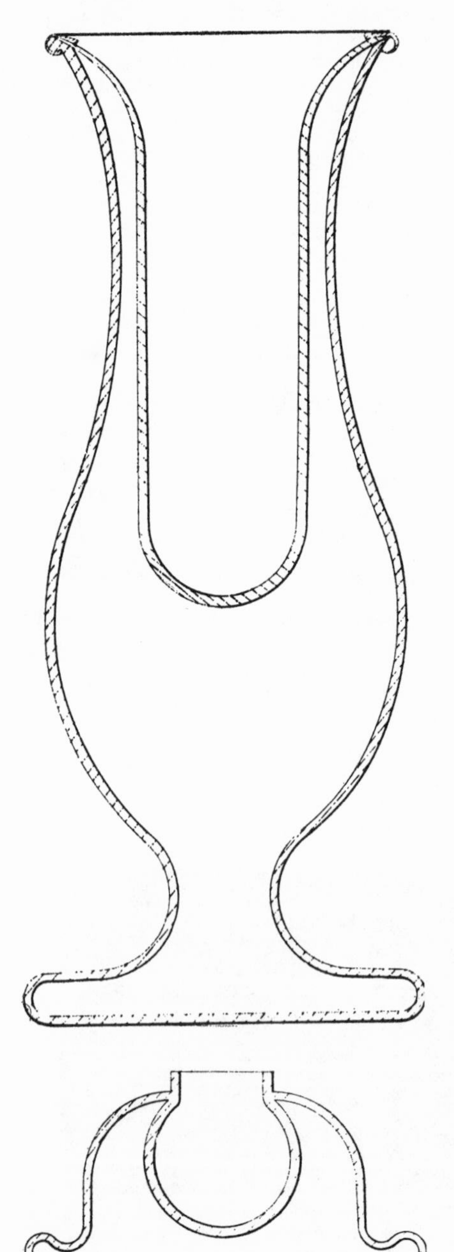

ON December 19, 1949, a process for the manufacture of the most beautiful silvered glassware ever made was patented by Frederick Hale Thomson and Edward Varnish, both of London, England. While this was not the first such patent for silvered glass issued in England or America, it was by far the most artistic accomplishment and was of the very best quality.

To produce their fine silvered glassware, Messrs. Thomson and Varnish had vessels of glass blown whose interiors were hollow (see illustrations from original patent papers, *left)*. The hollow spaces between the inner and outer walls of the vessels — goblets, mustard pots, inkwells, decanters, perfume bottles, mugs with hollow handles, flower vases, glasses, brush trays, pen trays, muffineers, smelling bottles, tea caddies, butter dishes, covers and plates, dishes, salt cellars, plateaus, wine coolers, bottle stands, cruets, etc. were silvered with a solution containing nitrate of silver, spirits of wine and saccharine. The glass articles themselves are believed to have been manufactured by James Powell & Sons of the White Friar glassworks in London.

Included in the patent papers was an interesting method for producing these hollow-walled vessels by joining together two pieces of glass—the inner and outer walls of the vessel—with a metal rim or seal which was fastened or bonded to the two pieces of glass with plaster of Paris. (See patent illustration, and vase from the Henry Ford Museum, pictured.)

Beautiful color effects were produced by plating the articles with colored glass and subsequently cutting through the colored plating to the crystal glass beneath with various kinds of designs in intaglio. For this purpose, brilliant shades of red, blue, purple, green and yellow glass were used as a plating over the crystal body glass. The dazzling effects such designs produced are far and above the usual type of silvered glass manufactured in the nineteenth century.

Left: Silvered glass vase, blue overlaid on crystal, and cut through in a design of flowers and leaves, inner and outer sections of the vase joined together at the rim with metal seal in accordance with the method outlined in patent issued to Frederick Hale Thomson and Edward Varnish; 7⅞" high; from the Henry Ford Museum, Dearborn, Michigan.
Right: Silvered glass goblet, green overlay cut to silver (clear) glass, made by E. Varnish & Company; from the author's collection.

Left: Silvered glass vase, blue overlay cut to silver (clear) glass, made by E. Varnish & Company; from the collection of Mrs. Irene Barbour.
Right: Silvered glass scent bottle, purple overlay cut to silver (clear) glass, made by E. Varnish & Company; from the author's collection.

"Ivory" Cameo Glass

by ALBERT CHRISTIAN REVI

Two views of vase in Webb's novelty-type cameo glass in imitation of old carved ivory, depicting "Tragedy" (above) and "Comedy" (below). Green and red enamels are used on leaves and berries about the neck; heavy gold encrustations on foot, neck and mask handles; 8" high.

ONE of the novelty-type cameo glasses which appeared in the last quarter of the 19th century was made in imitation of old carved ivory. The ware was produced by a process patented in England, November 30th, 1887, by "Thomas Wilkes Webb of Stourbridge Glass Works in the County of Worcester, Manufacturer." A patent covering this same process was issued to Mr. Webb in America and is dated February 19, 1889.

The method for producing this novelty glassware was stated very clearly by Mr. Webb in his specifications as follows:

"The object of the present invention is to produce a novel and highly ornamental effect in glass—viz., an imitation of old carved ivory.

"In the accompanying drawings I have shown a vase in the various stages of the process, Fig. 1 being an elevation of an opaque glass vase before the process is commenced; Fig. 2, a similar view showing the first stage of the process of ornamentation, and Fig. 3, a similar view showing the process completed.

"In carrying out my invention I take any desired form of article—say a vase—of ivory or white opaque glass *(see Fig. 1)* blown on molds or otherwise produced by usual glasshouse methods. Upon this vase I produce any desired pattern or design—a branch of the vine, for instance, with leaves and grapes *(see Fig. 2)* to represent the carvings on ivory, in the following manner: The vase is painted or printed upon with an acid-resisting substance and then submerged in hydrofluoric acid, which eats away the surface not so protected and leaves the surface beneath the resist in relief. This eating away of the ground by acid may be supplemented by cutting or engraving with a wheel or otherwise, to give additional prominence or delicacy where required; or in some instances the action of the acid will not be necessary—as, for instance, when it is desired to obtain the effect of sharp or deep carvings. The desired pattern having thus been produced in outline upon the vase, the acid-resist is entirely removed, and the veinings upon the leaves and other marks are produced by

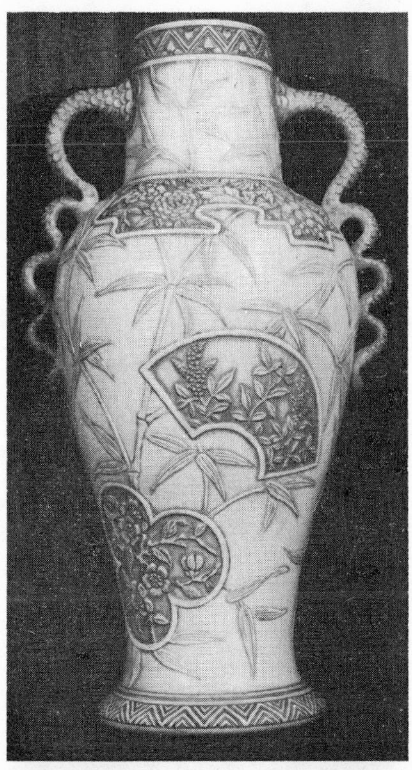

the wheel or graver *(see Fig. 3)*, the vase being then polished.

"The appearance of old carved ivory is produced upon the vase by tinting the same with brown or other suitable color, applying more color in some parts than in others, so as to give the effect of increased prominence to the prominent parts, as well as an aged appearance to the whole *(see Fig. 3)*. Thus the markings and the veins of the vine-leaves will receive a dark tint, which is readily applied and retained in the lines, and the prominent parts of the leaves and stem will receive and retain but little color. After tinting, the vase is fired to fix the color in any well-known manner.

"The effect produced upon an article of white opaque glass by treating it as above described is very striking and ornamental, and the imitation of old carved ivory is exceedingly close."

George Woodall and his brother Tom, master engravers for Webb, used old specimens of Indian, Chinese and other Oriental and East Indian objets d'art as models for this new conception of the cameo technique.

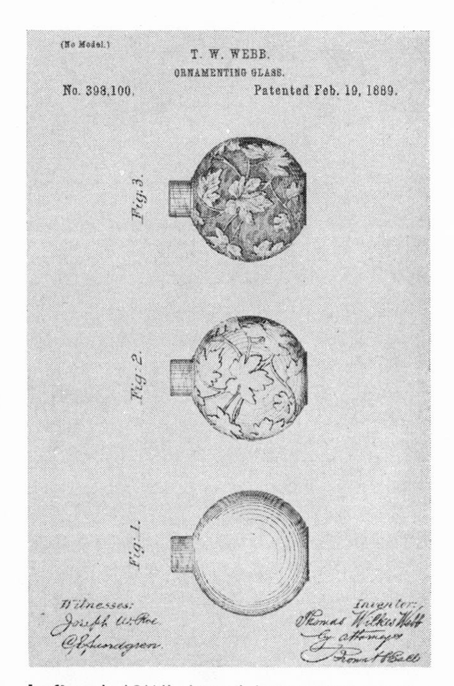

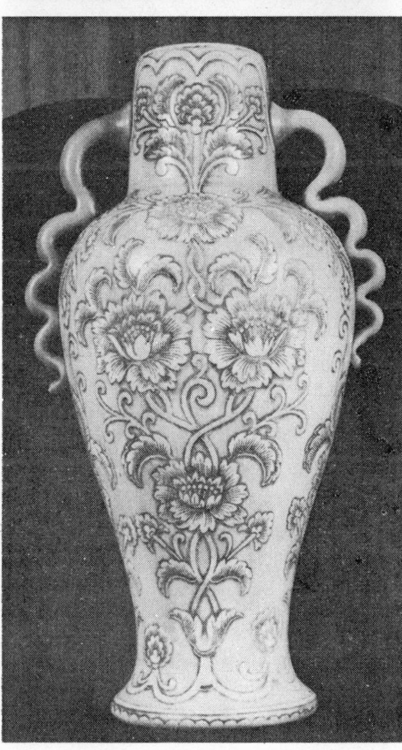

Left, pair 10¼" signed, ivory cameo vases in the Chinese manner, "Male" and "Female" (bamboo and floral respectively) designs. Louis Neiman collection. **Above,** Webb's patent filed in Washington, 1889.

Their first productions met with Royal favor and were purchased by Queen Victoria. Following Victoria's approval of this new ware production was stepped up considerably to supply the ever-increasing demands of the public.

Several designs for cameo glass articles made in imitation of old ivory are shown in the pattern and design books of Thos. Webb & Sons prefixed by the initial "K". To some it indicates that the designs were the work of a man named Kretschman, although it is known that Messrs. Barbe, Facer and Nash, all members of the Woodall Gem Cameo team, also produced designs for such wares.

The imitation of Oriental ivory pieces made according to Mr. Webb's specifications are not on a par with the earlier hand-worked and engraved cameo glass. The engraving wheel was used primarily to polish up details already blocked out with acids, and seldom does one find a specimen on which any fine detailed graving appears. The vases illustrated are some of the few of many pieces we have examined exhibiting any real merit.

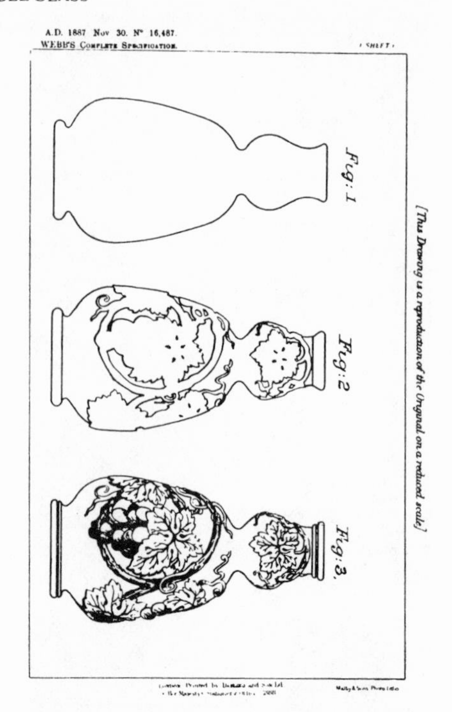

Webb's patent filed in London, Nov. 30, 1887.

Napoli Glass

by ALBERT CHRISTIAN REVI

ON May 22, 1894, Albert Steffin, head of the Mt. Washington Glass Company's decorating department, patented a new means for decorating glassware which the firm named "Napoli."

"The invention," states Mr. Steffin in his patent specifications, "consists in forming upon one side or face of the glass article to be decorated an outline of the figure or design to be produced, and forming upon the opposite side or face of such article the complete figure or design, whereby the outline thus formed upon one side will, by reason of the transparency of the glass, combine with the main body of the decoration upon

Palmer Cox's popular Brownies popped up everywhere in the 1890s, even on this fine Napoli glass covered jar! **Collection of Mrs. J. M. Miller.**

the opposite side, and produce a novel and peculiar effect."

Mr. Steffin stated also in his patent papers that the decoration should first be outlined on one side of the article to serve as a guide for producing the main body of the design upon the opposite side. This method was especially recommended in decorating hollow glassware — vases, bowls, jars, etc. Owing to the shape of such articles of hollow glassware, access to the interior is more or less difficult, and in many cases it is almost impossible to produce decorations upon the interior with any degree of accuracy. The outline of the designs on the exterior served as a guide in forming the main body of the decoration in colored enamels on the interior of the hollow vessel. In all cases, the effect of depth or solidity in the decoration produced by this method was due to the fact that the outline is upon one side of the glass and the main body of the design upon the opposite side. The result was a striking and novel effect, one that could not be produced by applying the entire decoration upon one side only of the glass.

A great practical advantage resulted from Mr. Steffin's new method for decorating glassware, since by it both the colored and the metallic gold or silver decoration could be fired at one firing. Heretofore, when both metallic and colored decorations had been employed in the production of a given design, both being applied to the same side of the glass and in contact with each other, it had been impossible to fire the article at a single firing, for either the metallic decorations would be absorbed by the colors, or would be so affected by the fumes arising from the colored enamel decoration in the process of fusing as to lose their proper color and brightness, and thus be practically spoiled. Consequently it was necessary to subject the article to two firings, applying the colored designs first and fixing them in the kiln before the gold or silver outline decorations could be added and fired at a much lower temperature. Readers familiar with the techniques of firing hand painted china will well understand the difficulties.

The covered jar shown in our illustrations is a fine example of Napoli glass. The design upon it portrays three Brownie figures, then at the zenith of their popularity. All of these figures are painted on the inside of the jar with colored enamels and in an exaggerated style. The costumes are in bright shades of blue, brown, green, red, and black; the stockings are a bright orange. On the outside of the jar, the outline of the figures has been done in gold tracery. In addition there is a network of interlacing gold lines decorating the entire surface of the jar. The silver-plated cover has a turtle finial and is marked on the under side "M.W." (for Mt. Washington). The name "Napoli" is painted on the base of the jar in black enamel lettering.

Mr. Steffin's patented technique for decorating glassware with enamels and gold does have an ancient origin in the so-called "reverse paintings on glass." Perhaps the most famous piece of ancient reverse picture painting on glass is the Paris plate, attributed to Antioch or Syria about 200 A.D. In the late 18th and early 19th centuries the technique reappeared in China where a brisk business in such wares was done with American and European merchants in the China Trade. Manifestations of the art can be found in European and American decorated mirrors and clock cases of the 18th and early 19th centuries.

It should be pointed out, however, that Steffin's added innovation (the outlining of the figures on the opposite face of the glass) does change the whole character of the decoration, making Napoli glassware different from its predecessors.

Ruby Glass

(Cranberry, Bohemian Red and Pigeon's Blood)

by ALBERT CHRISTIAN REVI

Miniature tea set in ruby (cranberry) glass, crystal handles and spout.

IN ancient times red colored glass was a rarity. The Egyptians produced a red glass with oxide of copper. Haematinum, or "blood red" glass, was also found in the Roman Imperial epoch; here, too, the coloring agent was copper oxide. By increasing the copper oxide in the glass batch, the ancients also produced a glass brick-red in color.

The first successful formula for a red glass closely resembling natural ruby color was given in Antonio Neri's *L'Arte Vetraria,* a book of glass recipes published in Florence, Italy, in 1612. Neri's formula for gold-ruby glass is often attributed to Johann Kunckel, a German glassmaker of the mid-seventeenth century. Kunckel's translation of Neri's recipe added no real improvement to the original formula, nor did the translation by Dr. Christopher Merret, an English physician, in 1662.

During these early years ruby glass was held in high esteem, mainly because of the exaggerated cost of production. Actually it cost little more to produce than many other colored glasses in spite of the ingredient gold being requisite.

In England, during the reign of William and Mary, a patent for producing "Red Chrystall Glasse," issued to Robert Hookes and Christopher Dodsworth, was validated June 12, 1691. In those days it was the prerogative of the throne to grant licenses to individuals to be the sole producers of various manufactured articles. This "patent" was not a new formula or recipe; it was merely a license allowing Messrs. Hookes and Dodsworth to be the sole producers of red crystal glass in England for a period of fourteen years.

Ruby glass covered compote, cut crystal knob, crystal foot and stem.

King George II issued a patent to Mayer Oppenheim on November 28, 1755, for the production of a gold-ruby glass. Oppenheim's formula listed "thirty grains of Gold" to every dissolved Dutch pound of "flint [glass] materials." After placing the material in a reverberatory furnace "a white flint glass [is] produced, which on being exposed to a second heat, will be the red transparent." The *Birmingham Gazette* for February 22, 1762, contained an advertisement to inform the public that: "Mayer Oppenheim, at his Glass-House on Snow-Hill, Birmingham, has to sell a large parcel of Lynn sand and fine white arsenick. *N.B. The Red Transparent Glass is to be had at the above Glasshouse, either in a light rose or deep ruby colour.*"

On October 20, 1770, Oppenheim received a patent from George III for "A New Method of Making or Manufacturing a Beautiful Opaque or Transparent Garnet or Red Glass."

Cranberry colored glass water pitcher with shell crystal handle.

Again he used "dissolved Dutch Gold," and added "Red Arsenick" and "magnesse" to make this opaque red glass.

The vogue for colored glassware was at a low ebb in the first half of the nineteenth century, public favor turning to white crystal glass, both cut and engraved. By 1865, the pendulum began to swing the other way. Jean Henri Chaudet of Rouen, France, a chemist by trade, patented a means for obtaining chrome salts used in the manufacture of red glass. Count Schaffgotsch of Schreiberhau, Germany, owner of the famous Josephine Glass Works, registered his patented means for producing in one melting a massive quantity of glass of a transparent red color so that objects could be made therefrom direct from the pot without flashing and without a second heating being necessary to bring out the color. To 3173 parts of other glass ingredients, Count Schaffgotsch added but 9 parts of red oxide of copper to produce a copper-ruby glass. True, this copper-ruby did not possess the pink and lavender tones of gold-ruby glass, but it was cheaper to manufacture, and the glass works at Josephinenhutte was noted for cheaper productions of more expensive glass techniques.

Franz Welz of Klostergrab, Bohemia, patented a method for producing still another type of ruby glass, using selenium. His "Process for Making Rose or Orange-red Stained Glass" is dated December 7, 1891. The "Creme Rose" and "Creme Orange" glass produced by Welz' method is quite orange in transmitted light and easily detected by even the unpracticed eye. (Selenium is the colorant used in the various imitations of Amberina seen in gift shops today.) Welz patented his method for coloring red glass in America on July 26, 1892.

On January 30, 1893, Mr. Welz again registered a patent for producing a selenium red glass. This time he added uranium salts and produced a reddish orange-yellow color when the light passed through it, and a greenish color when the light fell upon it.

Heinrich Ritter Von Kralik and Wilhelm Ritter Von Kralik, trading as Wilhelm Kralik Sohn, of Eleonorenhain, Austria-Hungary (Bohemia) patented a means for producing "Rose-red Glass." Their method closely resembles the Welz' formula for selenium-red or ruby glass. A patent was issued to this firm in America under the name of Alfons Spitzer, April 17, 1894.

Nikolaus Meurer of Cologne, Germany, patented his formula for producing a red glass from brown coal (lignite), December 11, 1900. The use of such a cheap material as lignite brought production costs to even lower levels. The red color was not a beautiful shade, but it was good enough for lamp globes and other commercial glasses.

Finally, on October 11, 1902, Rich-

Ruby glass mayonnaise boat.

ard Zsigmondy, a doctor of philosophy, residing at Jena, Grand Duchy of Saxe-Weimer, Germany, patented his means for producing pure gold-ruby glass for pressed, blown, and molded glassware. From 0.25 to 1.7 parts of gold in solution was added to every 10,000 parts of glass used; a rich ruby colored metal was produced. Gold is such a strong colorant that only a very small amount is needed to produce a large quantity of richly colored ruby glass. So intense is the color of true gold-ruby glass that a thin wine glass made entirely from this metal would be almost black in reflected light and somewhat opaque.

In the last quarter of the nineteenth century, ruby glass reached its zenith in popularity. Various methods for producing decorative and household wares in this popular color were employed. The most common means was to coat a ball of crystal glass with a thin plating or flashing of gold-ruby metal. This was accomplished in one of three ways: (1) by picking up the colored plating from a pot of molten metal; (2) by blowing the ball of crystal glass in a cup of gold-ruby glass; or (3) by taking up on the end of the blow-pipe a clod of ruby glass and working it onto the crystal bulb at the furnace. Sometimes the glass blower blew a small bubble of ruby glass and then coated it with a heavy casing of crystal glass. When the bulb was blown out to full size, the ruby glass would form a thin coat of red over the entire interior surface of the blow. In each case only a very thin coating of ruby glass was necessary to produce a richly colored article.

The several shades of ruby glass, ranging from a pale rose-pink, through the so-called cranberry shades, to those intense reds known as Bohemian-Red or Pigeon Blood, were determined by the thickness of the plating of ruby glass—the thicker the plating, the deeper the color.

Today the cranberry shades in ruby glass are the most popular, and collectors do not find it difficult to fill their many needs. In fact, so popular has this color become that it has given rise to reproductions by the score. New glassware fashioned after models of the late nineteenth century appears in gift shops from coast to coast.

It is difficult to positively attribute a piece of ruby glass to any one factory or locale. Being such a popular color, it was made in many glass factories in many lands. We come closest to a correct attribution by comparing the design and style of decoration used on ruby glassware with known types produced in other wares, but even this is uncertain. Unless the article is conveniently marked for positive identification, an "educated guess" is as good as an authority's pronouncement.

Nailsea Glass

by C. C. MANLEY

FOR WHAT IT IS WORTH, we will agree with the widely accepted premise that the Bristol area was the origin of Nailsea glass; there seems to be no evidence of it preceding the true Bristol blue of the 1780 period. Whether or not it had its origin in Bristol, one thing is certain—Nailsea-type glass had its birth in a bottle factory. Its evolution from simple stripes on bottle glass to the elaborate and magnificent specimens of the 1900 period is easily followed, but to associate certain pieces with individual factories is difficult. Associating specimens with the districts in which they were made is much easier.

We use the word "Nailsea" to describe a type of decorated glassware—not its origin. In the early 1800s Nailsea was a splashed glass, very different from what we associate the name with today. The application of the colors resembled the sploshed decoration found on early Bristol jugs, and since these jugs had all the characteristics of Bristol manufacture, Nailsea glass could easily have been associated with Bristol. Bristol was also a center for bottle and flask manufacturing.

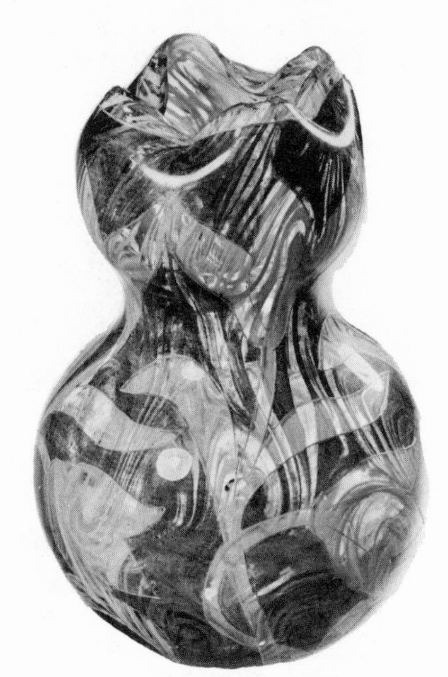

The stained pattern over the Nailsea type decoration on this vase adds little to its beauty. English, ca. 1900; 7″ high.

A cased glass jug, crystal over terra-cotta, sploshed with brown—very rare Stourbridge colors. The influence of early Nailsea glass is obvious. Stourbridge, ca. 1900; 3½″ high.

One remarkable feature of Nailsea glass is that throughout the 120-140 years of its so-called development, brandy flasks were the specimens on which new or improved decorating techniques were tried. Possibly the shape of the brandy flask lent itself as a trial horse for new colors and designs.

A similar development occurred in the manufacture of salt cellars. These unobtrusive objects were made in every glasshouse throughout Great Britain, firstly, to sample the metal before using it for other things, and secondly, to try out new colors and designs. In the author's opinion flasks were used for the same purpose.

As for the evolution of Nailsea glass, it runs with dates something like this: Shortly before 1800 there was the well-known crude bottle decorated with a haphazard design of colored stripes. Examples of this decorating technique can be seen in Bristol rolling pins, too. This was followed, about 1830, by articles in clear glass with colored stripes; few of these were made of lead glass. The years 1840-1845 saw the appearance of cased glass objects with nailsea-type decorations. Nailsea was now, it seems, a definite type to be pursued. The stripes and colors were put on in a regular manner, cased in crystal, and invariably worked off the pontil rod at the furnace.

After the 1851 Exhibition, we find pinched collars and pinched decorations added to the sides of various pieces. In 1885 or 1890 commenced what is known as the pull-up pattern. The colors and patterns were usually applied to an opaque body and cased over with crystal. This type of Nailsea glass is truly beautiful to look at and it demanded all the skill of the glassmaker.

Very early Nailsea glass, using common bottle glass as a base, could have been made at any of Britain's bottle works. Since there were hundreds of bottle manufactories in Great Britain —possibly thousands of these firms—

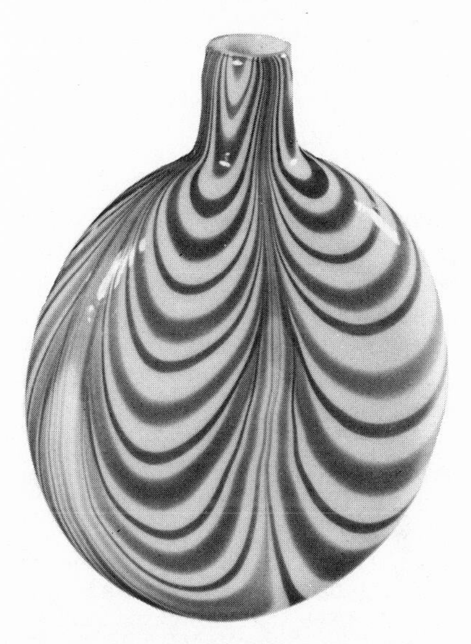

A typical Richardson Nailsea flask — red, white and blue drag loop stripes over a dense white base. (Red, white and green stripes were also used extensively.) This is not the pull-up threaded type, the colored decoration being applied by hand during manufacture. Stourbridge, ca. 1880.

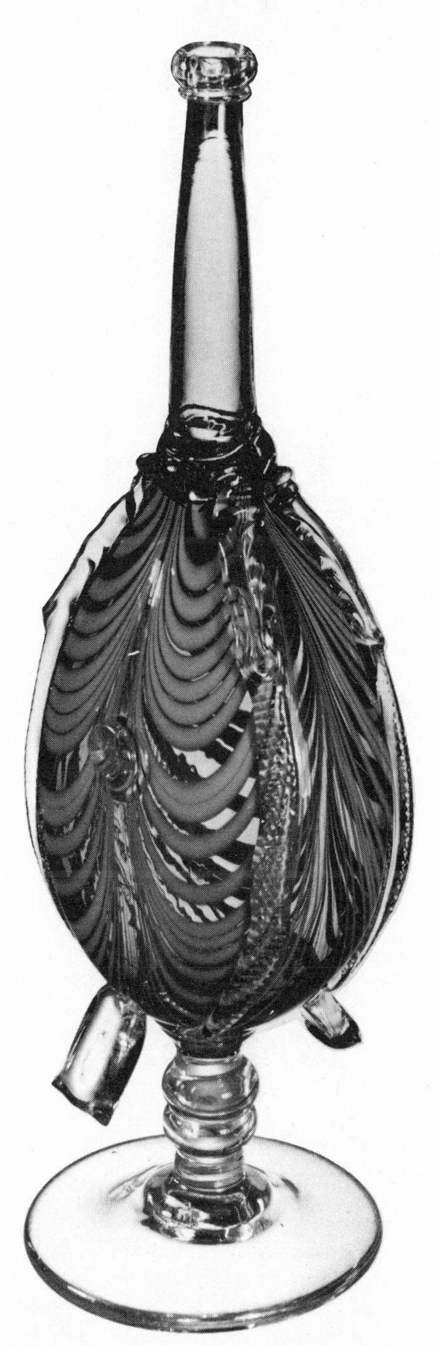

Bellows bottle; body stained ruby with white drag loop stripes; crystal foot and pinched and tooled decorations. Attributed to Warrington, but definitely North Country, ca. 1860; height 14 ½ inches.

A magnificent specimen of Stourbridge threaded glass developed from earlier Nailsea types. The lower half of the bowl is threaded with blue glass, the upper half with primrose-colored glass, all applied over a pull-up design of opal stripes; foot and welt of pinched crystal glass; ca. 1900; 4 1/2" high, 7" diameter across top of bowl.

we cannot attempt a true provenance, but when the pattern is applied to clear glass, the problem of an attribution is much easier. Our research into the place of manufacture has always, without exception, led to the North of England and included Warrington and Manchester. Time and time again, when we questioned the owners of such specimens, the answer was, "We had them from Warrington-or Manchester-or Edinburgh." In some cases Robinsons of Warrington were mentioned, or Molyneaux & Webb of Manchester, or the Alloa Glasshouse in Edinburgh. The Warrington Museum has some marked examples in their collection.

In the author's opinion the earlier cased specimens came from Birmingham, because both in the Birmingham Exhibition of 1849 and the London Exhibition of 1851, at least three Birmingham firms were showing Nailsea glass. So, too, were some Stourbridge firms, but here lies a difference, for although about 1860 the problem of bonding differently colored casings of glass was tackled in earnest, as late as 1870 all of the Stourbridge glass factories were having difficulties with multi-colored casings. Well after 1900, glassmakers in the Stourbridge District thought that only certain colors would bond together. This was proved wrong, but the combination of colors thought to be compatible by the Stourbridge glass manufacturers does help us to identify wares made in this area. Even after the reproduction of the Portland Vase in 1876, there was difficulty with the bonding of two different colored glasses. This leads us to believe that Stourbridge was a little backward in their technical knowledge of cased colored glassware.

After 1880 the situation changed. At that time John Northwood of Stevens and Williams produced the threading pull-up machines, this meant that the entire operation of casing and controlling the striped decoration was well under control. So it is safe to assume that glass exhibiting the "Nailsea" technique, numerous casings of glass, and elaborate patterns in pull-up threaded decoration was made after 1885, with possibly 85 percent of it emanating from the Stourbridge District.

With Nailsea-type decorations firmly established, we find glassmakers using these as a base for more elaborate pieces. Some were externally threaded using all colors; some had applied decorations; still others had enamelled decorations.

Another attempt to elaborate on Nailsea patterns was to stain another pattern over the one incorporated in the glass itself. This type of decoration is usually well done, but can only be described as "gilding the lily." With these later decorations, such objects cannot be dated much before 1900.

Some Nailsea-type glass with pull-up decorations similar to those made under John Northwood's patent by Stevens & Williams of Brierley Hill, England, was made on the Continent. These Continental pieces, most of which were produced in the Bohemian glass district, probably after 1900.

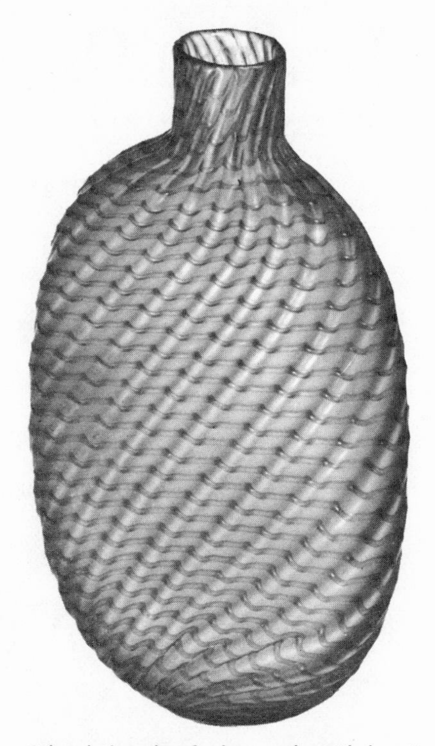

Colored threads of glass and swirled optic molding produce a very interesting effect in this Stourbridge flask (ca. 1890). The pattern was applied towards the end of manufacture and is not completely worked into the glass.

English Opalescent Glass

by C. C. MANLEY

A very unusual opalescent vase of excellent workmanship; green body with blue top. Stourbridge, ca. 1900; 5½" high.

TO ENGLISH collectors and dealers, opalescent glass is any glass which, on partially reheating, changes color.

The commonest color is very pale yellow, which when reheated, changes to a cloudy white. This color is governed to a certain extent by the amount of arsenic added to the original glass mixture.

The origin of opalescent glass in England appears to be very obscure. But it seems highly probable that once arsenic was added to glass (as a clearing agent) that the discovery of opalescence would not long be delayed. The use of opalescence as a decoration would soon follow.

Patents for opalescent glass were taken out around 1860, but it was certainly made before the Crystal Palace Exhibition of 1851 when it was shown by Messrs. Molineaux, Webb & Co. of Manchester, England. If it wasn't invented in a Midland works it was certainly developed in that region, especially in the Stourbridge area, for some truly magnificent art glass pieces were made there before the 1880s.

The common pale yellow opalescent ware is erroneously called "vasaline" glass, a name which is often used for Thomas Webb & Sons' "Lemonescent," for this glass has a vaseline glass, I feel it should be ap-

adding uranium to a high content arsenic mixture. But the correct name is Lemonescent and *not vaseline*. If collectors insist on using the name vaseline look which was obtained by plied to free blown specimens only, for at least they were individually made.

In the hands of a good chemist, practically all colors can be made to change when reheated. The most rare is blue. This was thought for many years to be unobtainable and, when discovered, was only made at very few glassworks.

Blue ribbed opalescent vase with applied crystal feet. Stourbridge (Richardson's), ca. 1890; 5½″ high.

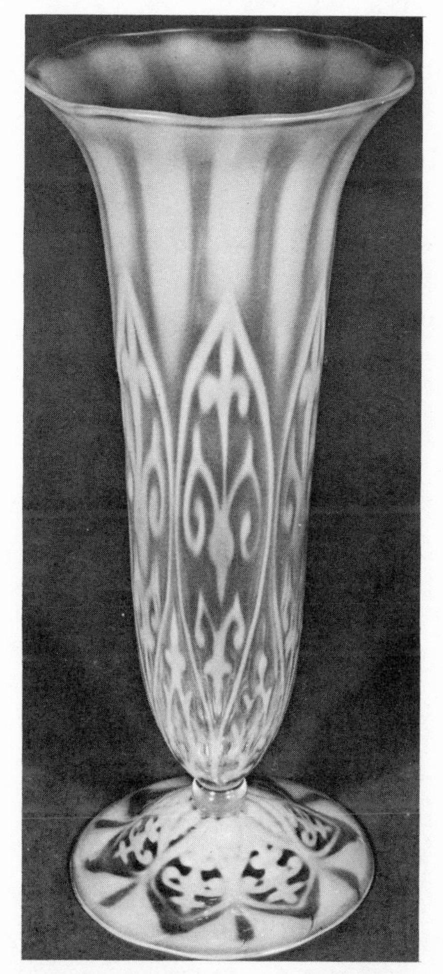

The style and pattern of this yellow opalescent vase suggests it was made by Stevens & Williams, ca. 1890; it also has affinities to Tiffany opalescent wares, ca. 1925. Height 14″.

Shape and surface taken together will generally identify the manufacturer, for most glass makers had their own surface patterns. The well-known "Horse Chestnut" pattern was exclusively Messrs. Richardsons of Wordsley until about 1936, when their moulds were sold to Thomas Webb & Sons of Stourbridge, who continued to use them, but with added uranium to their glass mixture. We therefore get Richardsons opalescent and Webbs Lemonescent both from the same moulds.

It is difficult to imagine a more delightful specimen of Webbs Lemonescent than their "Cascade" pattern, especially when gold ruby glass was discretely added as a decoration. Richardsons also had a cascade pattern about the same time as Webbs (1900–1910), but their glass lacked uranium and it looked rather anemic. The diamond pattern was not exclusively Webbs, but that pattern combined with their deep yellow coloring denotes its origin.

Trumpet shaped vases have always been popular with British glassmen, so it is natural to expect opalescent wares in this shape. Stevens & Williams appear to have produced a great quantity in this form, the surface patterns being ribbed to suit the design. But yellow opalescent glass was not exclusive to the larger firms, for this color was used by dozens of "Cribs" in the Midlands. Yet with close observation we can generally decide whether the product came from a crib. Very few crib products had a surface pattern, most were light in weight, and the shapes were always simple, and invariably the specimens were small.

The larger glasshouses of the Midlands produced some really fine art specimens in this glass at the turn of the century, but they were only the starting point for the more magnificent pieces. Some of these were partly or completely decorated with threads of all the colors of the rainbow. They had applied prunts, applied drops, and applied rims and feet in a variety of colors. Occasionally we find specimens with applied snakes and lizards. But of course, epergnes accounted for more opalescent glass than all the rest of the specimens put together. Iridescence over opalescent glass was tried, but it looked ghastly.

About 1900, Thos. Webb & Sons

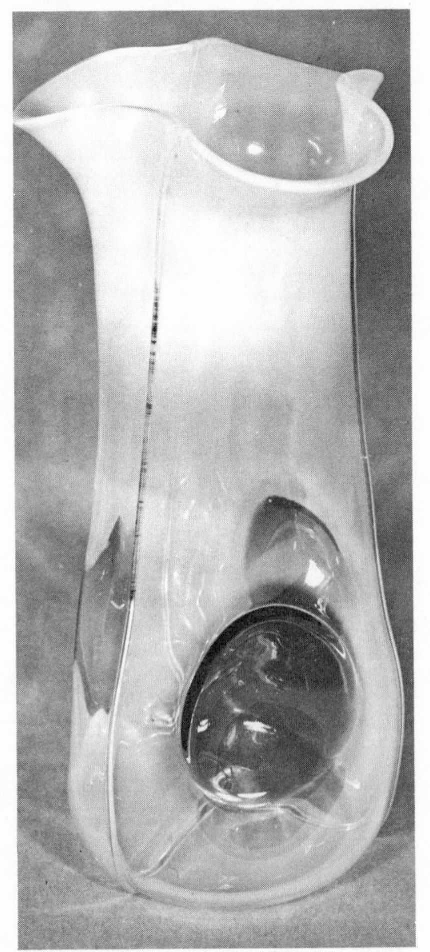

Yellow opalescent glass vase with three ribs and three bottle green indentations in base; extremely light in weight. Stourbridge (Thos. Webb & Sons), ca. 1900; 10½" high.

Webb's "Lemonescent" vase in the "cascade" pattern, the top decorated with a gold ruby lining. Ca. 1910; 8½" high.

made a very interesting type of opalescent glassware. The articles were generally plain in shape, and yellow in color. Heat was applied to the outside of the specimen only, leaving the perfect pieces with the outer surface white but with yellow inside. Unfortunately there seem to be more imperfect pieces of this type around, imperfect that is because of the patchy outer surface.

An extremely interesting situation occurs when we get away from the common yellow opalescent, for it seems that more thought and care was put into the design and production of opalescent wares of other colors. The results were some really startling specimens in adventurous designs which were particularly attractive. It is with the rarer colors that we find imagination and true workmanship. Certain articles in opalescent glass were made in two or more colors. This, of course, not only improved the beauty of the product but illustrates the skills being acquired by chemists at the beginning of the 20th century.

Pontils are of great assistance in the identification of English opalescent glass. Crib work (rarely collectable) never carried a ground pontil. Thos. Webb & Sons ground and polished the pontil of at least 90% of their specimens. Richardsons of Wordsley also ground and polished the pontils, but not in such quantity. Stevens and Williams made many examples with domed bases, which being awkward to grind, were generally left rough. The rest of the glasshouses in the Midlands used bases which needed no grinding.

Pressed ruby and yellow opalescent glass swan made by Burtles-Tate & Co., Manchester, ca. 1890; 4½" long.

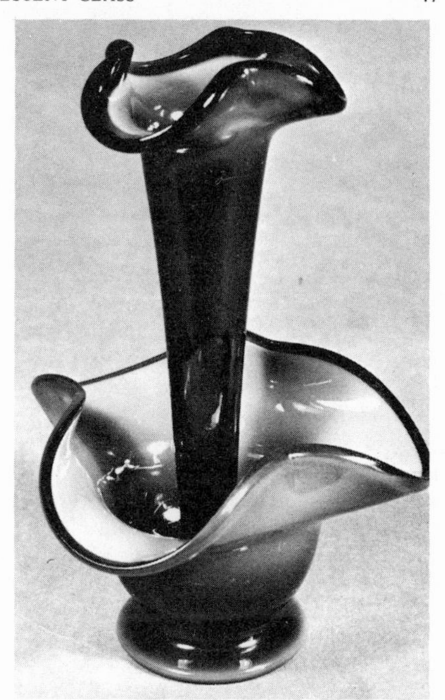

Dark blue vase with opalescent center. Stourbridge, ca. 1910; 5⅜" high.

Continental opalescent glass is somewhat of an enigma. The glassmakers must have thoroughly understood its manufacture, yet, other than opalescent glass and the way it was made. The operation of reheating obviously came up. He told me that when he had a specimen too big to re-enter the mouth of the furnace, he knew that he could get the same effect by waving the hot glass around in cool air outside the glasshouse. This, from someone who knew his job, is an illuminating comment on the manufacture of opalescent glass. Davidson's of Gateshead made a yellowish green cheap pressed glass, with the white edges. With the scarcity of good opalescent glass this is now being sold, possibly through ignorance, for vaseline glass.

I would like to record an interesting talk I had a few years ago with an old glassmaker. We were discussing

the small, cheap mantelshelf decorations, very little appears to have found its way to Britain, although undoubtedly special pieces were made. German "Annagelb" is not generally classed as opalescent glass.

The north of England has always produced the greatest amount of collectible pressed glass. That area probably produced the first opalescent pressed glass. Though an air of mystery surrounds English opalescent glass, pressed opalescent only adds fuel to the flames. In the late 1880s we find Davidson's of Gateshead taking out a patent for the production of pressed opalescent glass, yet ten years earlier a number of Tyne-side firms were producing it. In 1878, Sowerby's of Gateshead were in full production of crystal opalescent. Burtles-Tate & Co., Manchester, were producing both yellow and red opalescent swans in 1885. For some years after 1890,

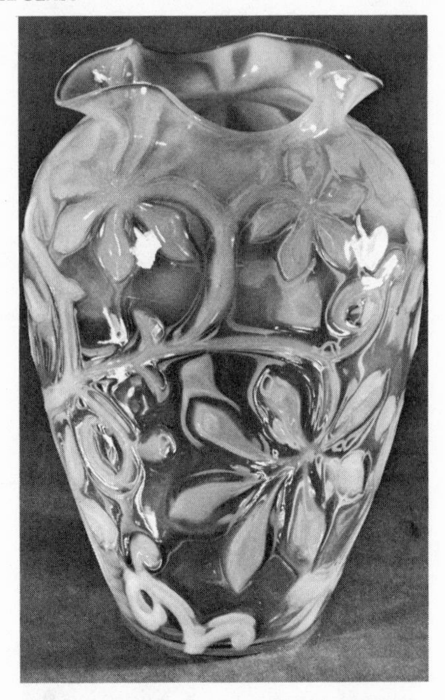

Pale "Lemonescent" vase in the Horse Chestnut pattern. Thos. Webb & Sons, Stourbridge, ca. 1936; 9" high.

Czech-Baroque Glass

by C. C. MANLEY

SOME TYPES OF GLASS are associated with definite localities, but Czech-Baroque glass was made not only in old Czechoslovakia, but in various places in Germany as well. The glass does not need to be of a special mixture; the colors do not follow a pre-arranged pattern; and the way of manufacture varies, too. It is the style which gives these wares their name; and though not actually a trade name, it is one which is still commonly used throughout the Continent to describe such wares.

There are three periods to consider in discussing Czech-Baroque glass. The years 1890 to 1900 are important, for it was during this period that the manufacturing technique, if not the styles, were being developed.

After the main period, 1910 to 1930, the second World War brought all artistic glass production to an end. With peace established, the glass manufacturers again began production of art wares and it was only logical that they would resume with some of the previously successful products. This third period, 1947 to the present, saw changes in styles and in manufacturing methods.

It was during the 1890–1900 period that distinct and definite types of glass were produced. One outstanding example was a glass named "Pandora." This name was patented, and the pride felt in this glass must have been extraordinary, especially when we realize that old Czechoslovakia was the cradle of decorative glass production. Pandora glass is reminiscent of Roman glass excavated at ancient burial sites. All kinds of Roman vessels were copied in this period, but very few could be finished at the furnace. Staining and special decorations were necessary to achieve perfection, and this made the products expensive.

Subjecting the object to various mineral vapors in a muffle gave

Pandora vase with threaded decoration about the neck in imitation of an ancient style in glass. Ca. 1890; 7¾" high.

Pandora jug-vase in an ancient style, with enamel decoration. Ca. 1890; 3¼" high. A larger size in this same design was also made.

Pandora jug-vase in mottled brown and rust, antique finish. Ca. 1890; 6½" high. Lagerberg collection.

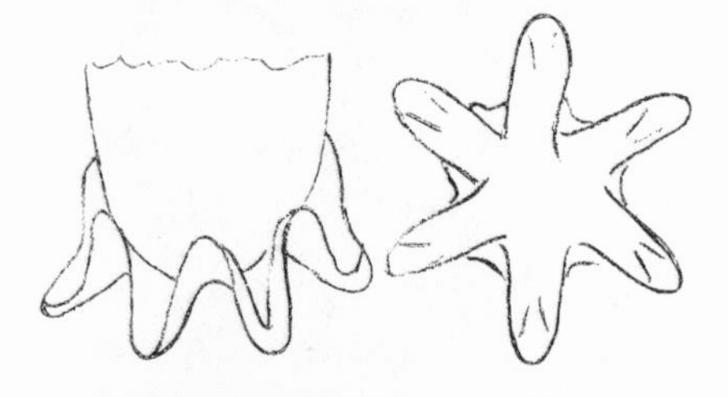

Right and left: Side and base view of an applied glass foot of a type commonly used on Czech-Baroque glass. A quantity of glass was applied to the base of an object, and from this the glassmaker pulled out as many appendages as were required.

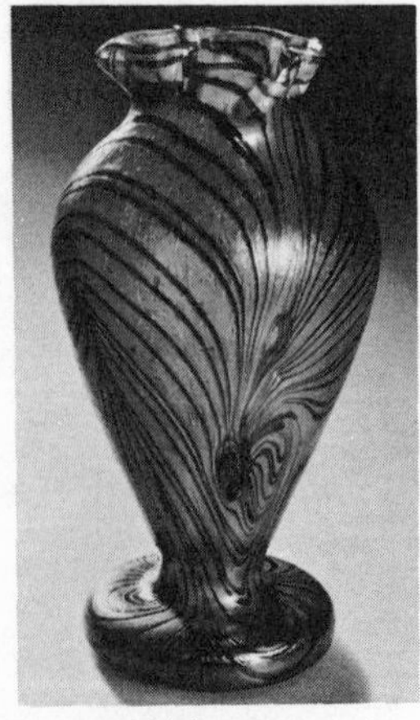

Iridescent glass vase copied from an ancient specimen found in the ruins of the Campanile in Venice, Italy. The hollow foot was formed from the original parison (blow). Ca. 1900; 8½" high.

Pandora glass an azure blue surface and a slight sheen. The variegated enamel decoration is representative of the Roman epoch, even to having breaks in outline to simulate age. A pontil mark will be found on all specimens. Compared with the Roman glass originals, the Pandora pieces are, if anything, slightly heavier. They were not produced in great quantities, and therefore are scarce.

This same period witnessed the production of an iridescent glass, not with a sheen but with a true iridescent surface, blue predominating. As their technical knowledge increased, other chatoyant colors were added to the glassmaker's palette. The first shapes used for iridescent wares followed ancient and medieval vessels rather carelessly. Very soon, edges were elaborately scalloped, then applied threads and appendages of glass appeared as part of the decorations. Iridescent glass was cheap to manufacture and made a good export line.

A very great percentage of the 1910–1930 period ware was definitely a glass of its time. Colors were gaudy and used with great abandon. Shaded colors were not often used, and every operation in its manufacture was cut to the minimum. All pontil scars were left untouched; the base of the object was kicked up to allow the vessel to stand firm; and the articles were exceedingly light in weight.

One outstanding feature of glass of this period is its outline. This has to be seen to be believed. The waviness of the edges is incredible. Some articles, such as bowls, are of little utilitarian value because of this characteristic.

Economy was the watchword. Even the hole in a fruit bowl (into which was screwed a stand) was pierced by the glassblower while the glass was in a plastic state. To add a little character, the wavy edges of an object were often trimmed with glass of another color. Any form of appendage, such as feet or handles, was applied in the same elaborate style.

The application of the feet on some glass articles invariably tells us the country of origin. The process most often used was to cover the base of a vase with a quantity of glass, and from this to pull out as many feet as were required. If the glass used for the feet was crystal, the pontil can be seen through the feet. When the foot was blown as part of the article, it was always hollow.

Handles, too, tend to show the country of origin. In Czech-Baroque pieces, they were applied more for ornamentation than use. If plain, the handles are always thin; if they were thick, it was only to have enough metal for the glassblower to pinch, crimp, and distort the handle into some fantastic form.

Decorations followed the same gaudy pattern. Flowers and leaves were perfect subjects to exploit. Some of the enameled decorations of flowers and animals found on these wares do not exist in real life. Large quantities of painted and gilded glassware were made without fixing the decorations in a kiln; and quite often these decorations have worn off over a period of years.

Although the whole production of Czech-Baroque glass was intended to be cheap in every way, the cooperation of the technicians and the skilled glassblowers produced amazing results. Towards the end of the true Baroque period in the mid-1930s, certain changes began to take place. The fancy designs lingered, but the glass adopted an English appearance. The Czech manufacturers, although they had embarked on a more substantial type of glassware, continued the cheap way of production, but the glass was heavier, making it better able to compete with the finer quality English glass.

As the style of the two countries—England and Czechoslovakia—began to assimilate, the difficulty for collectors to separate one glass from the other became obvious. The first definite break from tradition came with the hand-made crystal lampshades and vases in the form of flowers and leaves. The adoption of cased glass opened the field to unlimited opportunities. All that the English glass manufacturers had done, the Czechs did cheaper—Satin glass, Cased glass, Aventurine glass,

Satinglass ewer-vase with several Czech-Baroque characteristics—excessive wavy edge about top, a vertically flattened and crimped handle, a hollow foot, and rather crude enamel and gilt decoration. Ca. 1910; 10" high.

The elaborately pinched handle and uninspired enamel decoration, identify this crystal jug as a rather cheap piece of Czech-Baroque glass. Ca. 1910; 12" high.

Sploshed glass, Cased and Sploshed glass, and Marble glass—all types were imitated. But occasionally the Czechs developed something new.

Just prior to World War Two, experiments were being carried out on a type of glass which was sprayed with glass dust to form patterns and ornaments. With the coming of the war, all efforts in the European glass industry were diverted to other channels.

The war over, the glassworkers resumed experiments with this new decorating technique with great success. The result was opaque vases, sprayed with glass dust particles in varying sizes, and ranging in color from black to crystal. Flowers and leaves were the major design subjects, for these permitted great latitudes of formation. Some of the designs, after being applied, were burnt on; others were cased with crystal.

This art glass was difficult to make, but was splendid when finished. We do not think this glass was successfully copied by any other country. It may be that other artists, such as Tiffany in America, and Locke in England, had sown the seeds of this idea. Tiffany had already cased pieces of colored glass in crystal to form various designs, while Joseph Locke working for Hodgetts, Richardson & Son, had painted flowers and birds on opaque vases and cased them in crystal.

There are undoubtedly thousands of pieces of Czech-Baroque glass in many collections, their owners believing them to be English specimens. Any vase, bowl, dish, jug or decanter with any of the following characteristics is more than likely Czech—not English or American.

1. Excessive wavy edges; especially with a colored rim.
2. An elaborate form.
3. The pontil broken off and the base of the object kicked up. (Kicking up the base of the object obviates any need to polish the pontil mark; it also allows the piece to stand firm without grinding the base flat.)
4. A hollow foot formed of the original blow.
5. A vertically flattened and crimped handle.
6. Any glass with an exceptionally bright combination of colors—such as black and yellow.
7. Unnatural decorations with excessive gilt lines.
8. Feet made from one piece of glass and applied to cover the rough pontil.
9. Exceptionally light in weight in proportion to the size of the object.

All the aforementioned are the chief points to consider.

Overlay Glass— (Cut, Engraved and Etched)

by ALBERT CHRISTIAN REVI

THE art of producing the cased glass blanks necessary for cut, engraved or etched overlay glassware was known to the ancient glass workers, and can be traced back to a period between 100 A.D. and 100 B.C. when the Naples vase (*Figure 1*) was supposed to have been engraved. Many historians believe the engraving of glass cameos to be far anterior to this period, but for all practical purposes this approximate date has been accepted.

We cannot be certain of the method for casing or plating the cameo glass blanks used by the ancients but manifestly it must have been accomplished by one of two means: "cupping," whereby a bulb of glass of one color was blown into a cup of glass of another color made to receive it, or by dipping a bulb of glass of one color into a pot of metal of another color, thereby casing or planting the original bulb of glass with metal of a contrasting shade. Even today the possibility of producing a perfectly sonorous cased glass article is problematical, and in ancient times, when the law of coefficients of expansion and contraction in glasses was almost unknown, the mortality rate on cameo glass blanks must have been high.

Engraved cased colored glassware was manufactured in England in the 18th century. On November 22, 1780, William Peckitt of York received a royal patent from King George the Third for manufacturing cut and engraved cased colored glass. Peckitt's specifications required that "the glass maker gather a required quantity of uncouler'd glass, either crown, flint, or any other sort, from the melting pot while it is flexibly hot, which glass must then be marbled level and smooth; then immediately he must gather upon that, over the whole or any particular place or places, a quantity of coloured or stained glass of the same temper from another pot, which in like manner he must marble, blow, and spread level and smooth, heating in again the same as often as occasion shall require." Peckitt also suggested that

FIGURE 1

FIGURE 2

FIGURE 3

the colored bulb could be gathered first and coated with uncolored glass in the same manner.

"The glass cutter," continued Peckitt, "by his apparatus of wheels and other instruments (as commonly used), with water, or oil, and emery, must grind off so much of the coloured glass from the uncoloured glass, which must appear in ornamental devices in parts, polishing the same with oil, tripoli, and putty, as his ingenuity shall dictate." The finished product must have looked very much like the engraved beaker of ruby overlay glass shown in *Figure 2*.

On November 25, 1853, Emanuel Barthelemy, Tony Petitjean, and Jean Piere Bourquin, all of London, patented their means for etching through cased colored glass to various depths to produce a shaded colored design. By using cut-out stencils, a design was painted on the colored surface of the glass article with resists. Hydrofluoric acids etched away the exposed portions of the glass (those parts not covered by the resist) leaving a colored design in relief. Portions of this raised colored design were thinned down with acids, producing shaded colored patterns on a background of clear glass or glass of another color.

Benjamin Richardson of the Wordsley Flint Glass Works, near Stourbridge, patented his process for etching relief designs on cased colored glass June 20, 1857. His process more or less paralleled the Barthelemy-Petitjean-Bourquin patent except that

FIGURE 4

Mr. Richardson suggested the use of guttapercha as a resist.

Stevens & Williams of Brierley Hill manufactured beautiful intaglio engraved cased colored glassware in the last quarter of the nineteenth century. The small vase with engraved mushrooms shown in *Figure 3* is in purple glass over rose and with a base color of ivory. Similar wares in transparent rose, blue, and green over ivory colored glass were produced. Joshua Hodgetts was the engraver most prominently associated with this type of engraved colored glassware at the Brierley Hills Glass Works.

Bohemian glass manufacturers were responsible for some very choice pieces of cut and engraved cased colored glassware. The art developed in this area of Europe about the middle of the seventeenth century and continued to be a favorite type of glass embellishment far into the nineteenth and twentieth centuries. There is little to distinguish Bohemian cut overlay glasswares from those made in England and America from 1830 to 1880 and collectors will always be at variance with one another over a correct attribution.

Some of the most artistically engraved pieces of overlay glass came from the factory of F. Steigerwald in Munich, Germany, about 1855. The principal artist engaged by this factory was F. Zach. Zach's designs were engraved in colored relief, usually a deep blue, on crystal glass. The outer casings of colored metal were so skillfully thinned down that the subtle color gradations produced superb pictorial effects. (*Figure 4*) Examples of Mr. Zach's work are to be found in the Brierley Hill Library collection, the Victoria and Albert Museum in London, and in many private collections all over the world.

FIGURE 5

The monumental covered pokal shown in *Figure 5* was engraved in Bohemia by Karl Pfohl about 1865. The triple cased glass—blue, over white, over crystal—has been expertly engraved with Pfohl's favorite subject, horses, in a style very similar to Zach's. However, Pfohl's works lack the superb details found only in Zach's productions.

The technique of cutting and engraving cased colored glassware was a more or less universal art practiced in most European and American glass factories between 1830 and 1880. Definitely much engraved or cut overlay glassware was produced at the Boston and Sandwich Glass Company, but we can be certain similar wares were manufactured at other American factories as well. Lura Woodside Watkins in her *Cambridge Glass* mentions the beautiful work of Louis Vaupel and Henry Leighton, as well as others prominent in this endeavor at the New England Glass Works. She also quotes from a letter written to Thomas Gaffield by William Leighton, Jr. describing in detail a magnificent vase composed of four layers of glass that was cut and engraved by his father at the "New England."

Searching for a cheaper means for obtaining the same effect as produced by cutting and engraving cased colored glass, the Atterbury brothers, James and Thomas, and James Reddick patented a means for pressing and blowing articles of glass with raised colored designs on a crystal ground. Three patents covering their processes were issued in America, one on March 4, 1862 (also registered in England April 26, 1862), and two issued on June 3, 1862. In each case the first step was to press a colored glass design in a figured mold; after releasing the plunger, the glass

Cut overlay glass cream pitcher, dark blue over white, or crystal. Encrusted with gold decorations. American or European c1840. ***Author's Collection.***

worker blew into the mold a bulb of colored or uncolored glass to which the pressed design adhered.

Benjamin Bakewell, Jr. took this process a step further when he patented his "Double Glass" on Sept. 29, 1874. Bakewell's process produced the same type of glassware entirely by a pressing operation. On November 9, 1880, William L. Libbey registered his patent for pressing cameo glass which, in many ways, resembled Bakewell's and Atterbury's processes.

Although they seldom ever resemble cut and engraved overlay glassware, the shaded opalescent glasswares—Spanish Lace, Spot Resist, Opalescent Hobnail and similar patterns designed to produce a raised white design on a colored or uncolored ground—were attempts to emulate this type of ware.

Silveria Glass

by ALBERT CHRISTIAN REVI

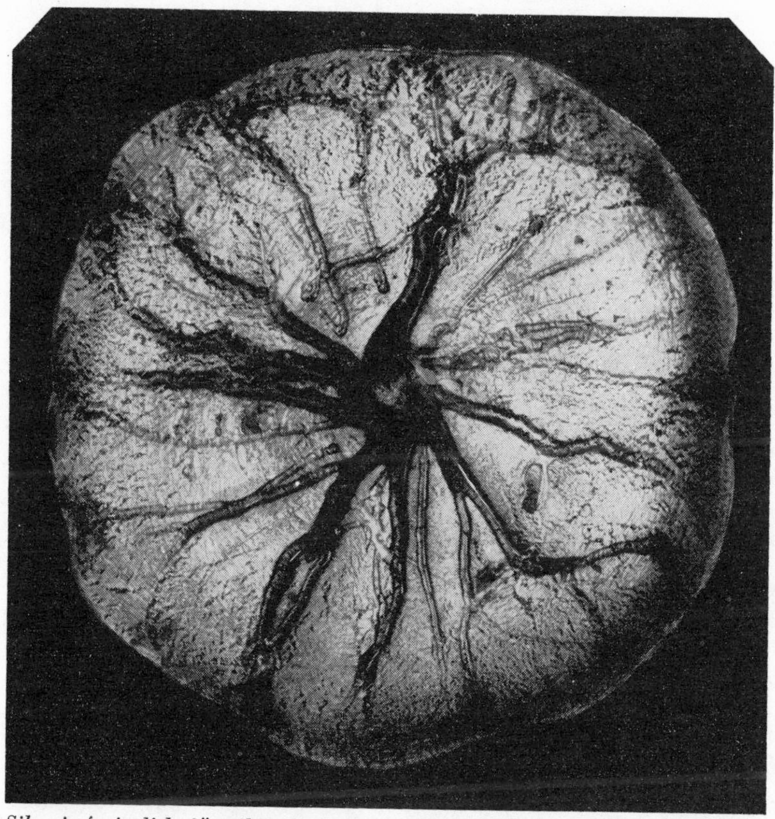

Silveria fruit dish, 9"; silver leaf coating tinted with transparent amethyst and gold, green trailings from center. Borough of Stourbridge Glass Collection.

SOMETHING akin to the *fondi d'oro,* the gold sandwich glass of ancient times, was produced by Stevens & Williams, of Brierley Hill, England, at the turn of the century. Its inventor, John Northwood II, named it "Silveria". In our talks with Mr. Northwood in his home at Brierley Hill some years ago, he told us that he developed this type of silvered glassware about 1900; his father was not in good health at the time but nevertheless was present in the shop during the experiments lending encouragement and helpful suggestions.

Silveria was made by sandwiching silver foil between two layers of transparent crystal or colored glass. The trick of production lay in the fact that the primary bulb was blown to almost full size before the foil was picked up from the marver. A protective film of glass was then placed over the foil by dipping the bulb into a pot of fluid metal. Trailings of colored glass were dripped here and there on the surface of the article sometimes haphazardly, sometimes with purpose of design.

Mr. Northwood's Silveria would seem not to be a unique type of glassware for as early as February 13th, 1878, Paul Raoul de Facheux d'Humy, of Litchfield Street, Soho, County of Middlesex, patented a somewhat similar means for decorating glass.

Mr. d'Humy's method differed from Northwood's in that the primary bulb was not blown to full size before picking up the silver or gold foil from the marver; consequently, when the parison was expanded to full size the foil imprisoned between the two layers of glass tore apart giving a somewhat different effect than Silveria.

Still another patent for applying metals in the manufacture of glassware was registered in England on November 29th, 1878, through a patent attorney, under the name of Messieurs Monot, Pére et fils, and Stumpf, of Paris, France. This invention related to a process of applying a layer of gold or other metal foil either between two layers or thicknesses of glass or crystal, or on the exterior thereof, for the purpose of producing the ornamental effect known in France as "chiné metallique".

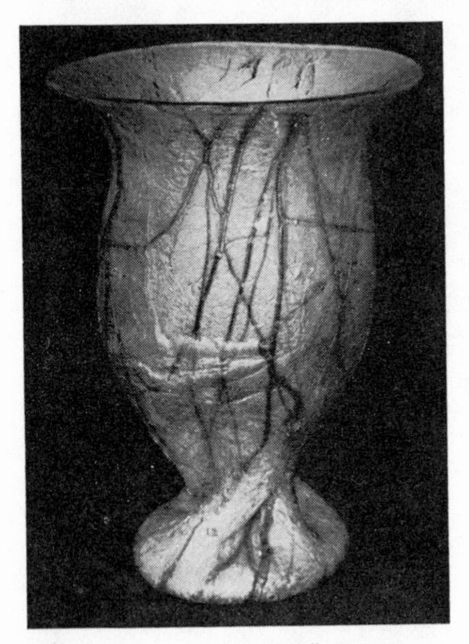

Silveria vase, 8½" high, 6" across top; flanged body, twisted four pillars at base; silver leaf coating tinted with rose and pale blue, green trailing tendrils all over.

Several methods for the manufacture of this ware were suggested in the patent specifications. The only real difference between Messrs. Monot and Stumpf's and d'Humy's processes was that the former suggested making the outer shell first and coating the inside of this "envelope" or "cap" of glass with the metallic film, then blowing inside of this envelope an inflated gather of glass to seal the metallic substance between the two layers of glass. Further expansion of the metallized bulb resulted in the tearing of the metallic sheet or coating between the layers of glass, producing the effect mentioned in d'Humy's specifications.

The decorative techniques sug-

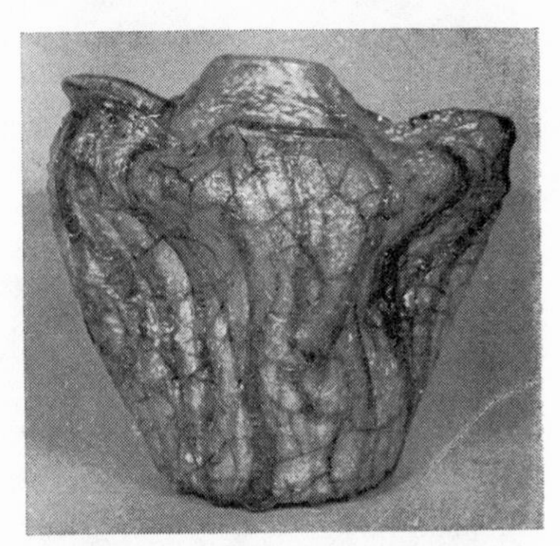

Small experimental "Silveria" vase by John Northwood II; trailings of emerald green and yellow on a transparent crystal-silver ground. Author's collection.

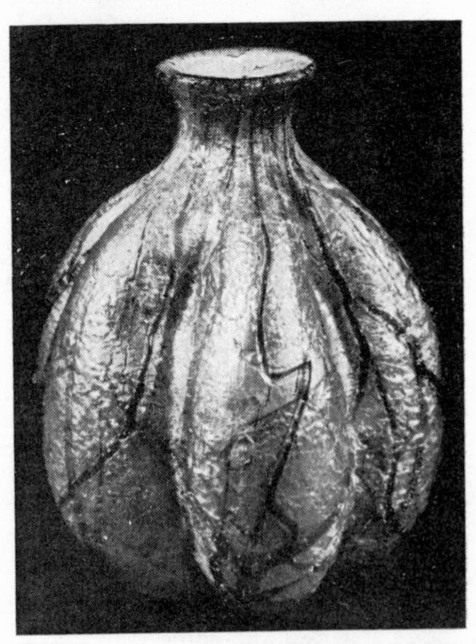

Silveria vase, oval 6-lobed body, 5" high; silver leaf ground with trailings in relief of bright green. Collection of Glass at the Brierley Hill Public Library.

gested in the d'Humy and the Monot-Stumpf patent papers were used to some extent by the exponents of *l'art nouveaux*. Gallé, Rousseau, the brothers Daum, and others introduced sheets of silver and gold foil within the walls of their many skinned glasses with some very interesting and beautiful results.

One factor on which all of these various wares depended for their lasting beauty was air-tightness. No cracks could occur in the outer or inner skin of the article or the exposed metallic foil, especially the silver foil, would oxidize and discolor. The small experimental piece given this writer by Mr. Northwood (above) has many such fissures in its outer surface; consequently it is now somewhat discolored wherever these crackles appear.

Pieces of Silveria are sometimes found marked "S & W" for Stevens & Williams. Mr. Northwood never patented his Silveria. In spite of its necessarily high production costs Silveria was a good seller and collectors should have no trouble finding specimens of this handsome glassware.

French Cameo Glass

by ALBERT CHRISTIAN REVI

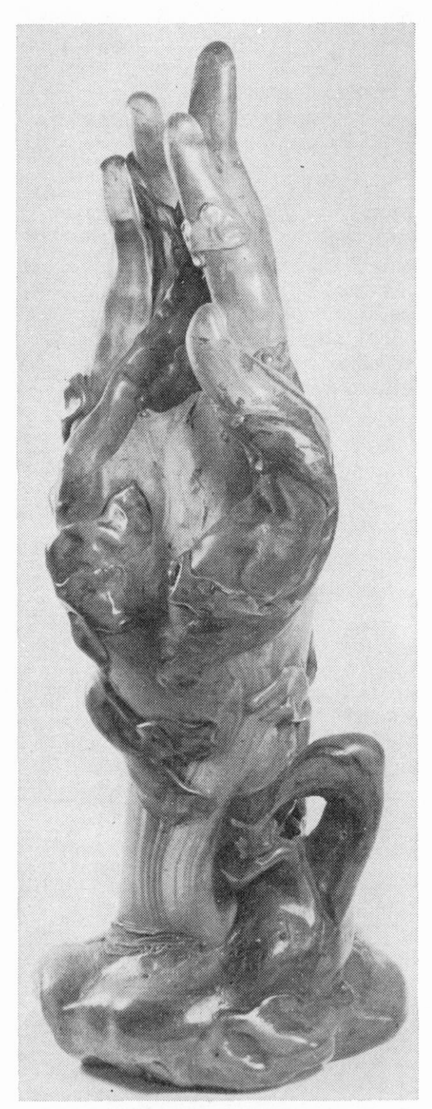

Cameo glass study of Nature's Hand, by Emile Galle.

THE FRENCH technique of acid engraving cameo relief designs on blanks of cased colored glass was but one facet of the trend in glass manufacturing known as "*l'art Nouveau,*" which became popular in France about 1880 and continued in favor until just before the first World War in 1914.

Cameo glass in the French tradition was not intended to rival the meticulously engraved English cameo glass. It was, instead, a new conception of glass design, utilizing color and form in what was originally intended as a subtle Oriental style, and very handsome and artistically executed examples were developed. French glassmakers were proud of their work, and almost all of their pieces bear a signature. Toward the end of the *Art Nouveau* era, the cameo glass, of such merit in earlier years, deteriorated into grotesquely formed pieces of garish colored glass.

BROCARD

Joseph Brocard, artist, glass technologist, and early disciple of *l'Art Nouveau,* exerted a strong influence on the work produced by such men as Galle, Rousseau, Marinot, DeLatte, De Vez, and many of his contemporaries. Primarily, though, Brocard was noted for his enamelled glassware, made in imitation of Oriental and mid-Eastern wares. Best remembered of these are his lighting fixtures, resembling enamelled Mosque lamps.

GALLE

The most renowned of the French masters of cameo glass was Emile Galle, who was born in the important glass center of Nancy, France, in 1846. Galle started his first glass factory in Mysenthal (Meisenthal), a small glass manufacturing center in the Moselle Department, in 1879. The blanks made at Mysenthal were decorated under his personal supervision in a small studio which he established in Nancy. His work gained public recognition at *l'exposition de l'Union centrale des arts decoratifs,* Paris, 1884. Galle's fame became such that he was appointed head of the School of Arts at Nancy. He developed to be the foremost exponent of the so-called "Art Nouveau," the

Cameo and enamelled oval vase by Daum Brothers; 4" high by 6½" long; aquamarine glass enamelled with white and green.

Portrait of Emile Galle by Victor Prouve.

Cameo glass pitcher by Emile Galle.

Scenic cameo and enamel vase by Le Gras, cameo and enamel work in natural summer colors.

modern style in glass in his time.

Galle took for his subjects flowers and landscape designs instead of the figure subjects shown by the English artists in cameo glass. By the use of varied colored casings of glass upon a base of either transparent or translucent metal, he obtained new and artistic effects. Some of these casings of colored glass were obtained by picking up colored glass were obtained by picking up powdered glass from the marver as the hot glass was being rolled to give it shape, re-heating the whole—in some instances this color was locked in by casing another layer of a different color over the entire mass—and finally blowing it into the shape desired. Galle utilized these masses of color underneath and on the surface of the glass by designing subjects to suit the object in hand, using the various layers of color in his flowers, insects, and landscapes. When we consider that all of this work was done in relief, by first etching out the mass with acid and then engraving the detail with the wheel, the craftsmanship underlying such beauty of individual work is apparent.

Galle's work, bought by museums and people of good taste in Europe and America, placed glass upon a high artistic plane.

Principal among Galle's collaborators and workers were Louis Hertaux who created several designs for him at Nancy, decorator Paul Nicolas, and August Herbst and Daigueperce, two of the most accomplished etchers and engravers in the Galle Studios. Paul Nicolas in later years worked for *l'Verrerie de la Compagnie des Cristalleries de Saint Louis,* a branch of the Baccarat firm, and under his own name in Nancy as a decorator of glass, exhibiting in the expositions of 1927 and 1937 and winning awards both years for his glassware.

After the death of Galle in 1905, the factory was under the direction of Victor Prouve until 1914. The wares produced during Prouve's management are marked with a star preceding the name "Galle". (This refutes undeniably the erroneous assumption by some dealers and collectors that pieces so marked were made by the hands of the master,

Left: Cameo glass inkwell by Daum Brothers of Nancy, France. **Right:** Russian cameo glass vase, ca. 1909.

Galle.) Following the first World War, 1918, the firm carried on production at Epinay in the Vosges mountains. The works changed hands in 1921, continuing for a time, but the glassware became increasingly poor in quality.

ROUSSEAU

Eugene Rousseau (1827-1891) worked originally in ceramics; later, he manufactured artistic glassware. He and Galle were the principal apostles of the new conception of glass design inspired by Japanese art forms, Japan being at that time just recently opened to the West. Among his other commendable wares were crackleglass, marbled glass, agate glass, and imitation gems. Rousseau sometimes encrusted his models with gold and introduced gold and other metallic oxides in his melts (glass batches). His first productions—and some consider these his best—date from 1867 when he was employed by the Appert Brothers of Clichy. After gaining recognition at the exposition of 1884, Rousseau sold his establishment to Leveille in 1885.

LEVEILLE

M. Leveille directed and operated a decorating establishment for glass and porcelain in 1869. In 1885, he acquired Rousseau's glass works and continued to make glass, as Rousseau had done, along lines inspired by Japanese art. About 1889, he produced glassware employing acid etching and wheel engraving in the style of *l'Art Nouveau.* At the beginning of the 20th century the business was taken over by Harant and Guignard of Paris, who were primarily decorators of glass.

MARINOT

Maurice Marinot, an accomplished painter, entered the glass trade in 1911 at Bar-sur-Seine, an ancient town pleasantly situated on the left bank of the Seine, about 125 miles south-

Cameo glass wine jug with silver gilt mountings.

east of Paris. His first productions were decorated with colored enamels; usually in designs of decorative flowers, birds, or feminine heads. From enamels he turned to deep geometric engraving, using blanks that were, to say the least, uninspired in form and color. In his third period, Marinot renounced exterior decoration for his glassware and, like Rousseau and Galle before him, sought colorful effects with the aid of mineral stains, oxides, and cased colored glass.

In later years Marinot developed a style all his own. Handling the blowpipe himself, often in the very doors of his furnace, he made those glass

Cameo glass teapot by Benjamin Richardson, circa 1857.

productions that won him honors during the Exposition of Modern Art, 1925, and won him the reputation among his countrymen of possessing the greatest genius of any of the craftsmen in glass.

DAUM

The Daum brothers, Auguste and Antonin, were originally from Lorraine, which probably accounts for the Cross of Lorraine used in their monogram. They founded their first factory in Nancy in 1875, producing bottles. Their earliest efforts in artistic decorative and tableware were with gold ornamentation; then they turned to

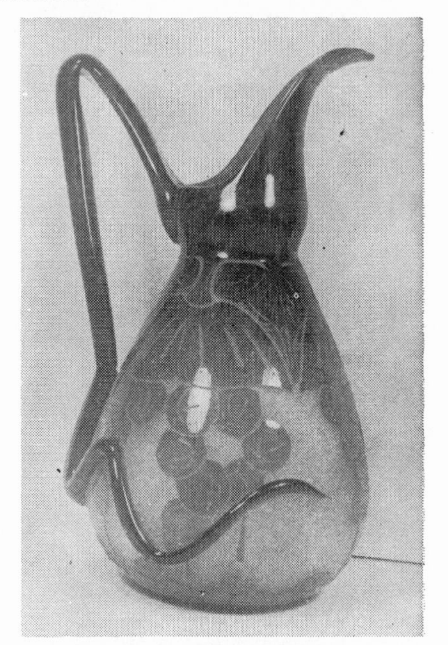

Rare cameo glass pitcher signed "La Verre Francais."

glassware inspired by Arabian designs and decorated with scrolls and gold leaves. Shortly after the introduction of this "Egyptian" glass, they began to produce colored glass by the "flushed" process. Their cameo and enamelled glasswares, produced about 1890, rank among the best representations of these types. The Freres Daum were active in the School of Art in Nancy during Galle's direction of that institution and also under the new staff formed in later years by Marinot. As time went on they developed techniques of their own which are familiar to us today. Currently the Daum glassworks is producing decorative crystal glassware in the modern vein.

OTHER FRENCH ARTISTS IN CAMEO GLASS

There were many lesser known, but nonetheless worthy, artists who worked in what is now termed "French cameo glass".

DE VEZ, who was associated with a glassworks at Pantin, northeast of Paris, about the beginning of the 20th century, had a penchant for beautiful colors and floral designs which made his productions noteworthy.

Cameo glass vase by Le Gras.

LE GRAS was noted for his imaginative glassware and bottles until he ceased production about 1914. He started work in Saint-Denis, a suburb north of Paris, in 1864. Especially laudable are his scenic productions.

MULLER BROTHERS of Luneville began their careers working for Emile Galle. They founded their own factory in the vicinity of Luneville, just south of Nancy on the Moselle River, afterwards moving it to Croismare. Cameo pieces made at Luneville are signed *Muller, Muller Luneville,* or simply *Luneville.* Those made at Crois Mare bear the name of the town in connection with the name Muller or just *"Crois Mare."* Their most active period was between 1905 and 1937.

WILLIAUME, a Parisian artist, was noted for his acid-engraving on cased glass blanks, especially portraits, about 1878. Very few of his early portrait pieces have been found.

ANDRE DELATTE established his works in Nancy in 1921, the principal output being lighting fixtures and opaque glassware in imitation of the Bohemian opaline. Among his best wares were his cameo productions, often done with a sensitive combination of graceful design and vibrant color effects.

EDWARD MICHEL was the finest engraver of glass in France in his time. (He was a direct descendant of Nancy-born Claud Michel, 1738-1814, known as "Clodion", whose ceramic figure modelling was world re-

Sculptured cameo glass vase by Edward Michel.

nowned). Towards the end of the 19th century, Edward Michel worked for Rousseau and later Leveille. Examples of his cameo work are very rare. The quality of Michel's engraving rivals that of his English contemporaries, Woodall and Northwood.

M. WALTER of Nancy began working about 1925 in cameo glass and artistic productions of *pate de verre*. His cameo glass pieces are not always fine in color or design, but happily there are plentiful exceptions.

ALPHONSE G. REYEN was one of the most able engravers and decorators of glass, working for Eugene Rousseau about 1877. Many examples of his cameo work were exhibited at the exposition of 1889.

TESSIRE du MOTAY, KESSLER, and MARESCHAL were three artists who utilized the etching needle in making shallow cameo relief designs on glass, working from about 1862 until the end of the 19th century.

FRENCH STYLE CAMEO GLASS IN ENGLAND

Cameo glass in the French style was produced in most of the countries of Europe contemporary with the birth of this expression of *l'art nouveaux* in France. Benjamin Richardson of the Wordsley Flint Glass Works near Stourbridge, England, patented a method for producing cameo relief designs on a cased glass blank June 20th, 1857. Mr. Richardson coated the surface of a cased blank with gutta percha or india rubber, both resistant to acids, and removed some of the pellicle with a suitable tool before dipping the article in acid to remove those portions of the outer casing not protected by the resist. The article, being composed of two or more casings of colored glass, when finished displayed a design of one color in shallow relief on a ground of another hue. Mr. Richardson maintained in his specifications that the use of fluoric acid would leave a mat finish on the design, while a combination of fluoric and sulphuric acids would leave a bright finish.

On June 19th, 1885, Archibald Cochran of the Saint Rollex Flint Glass Works, Lanark, North Britain, patented a similar method for producing cameo relief designs on lamp globes. Mr. Cochran etched a relief design on the inner colored casing of his lamp globes leaving the outer surface smooth to the touch.

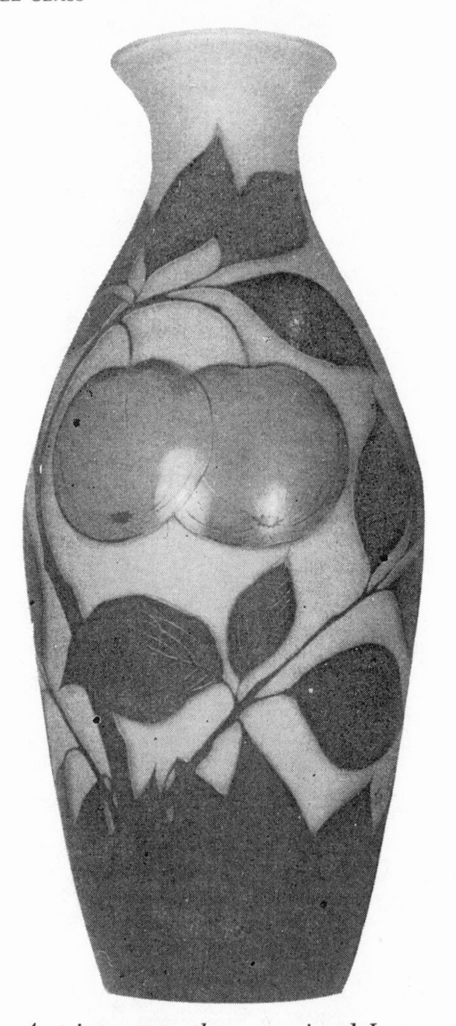

Austrian cameo glass vase signed Loetz.

Ludwig Kny, the son of Frederick Kny, a celebrated engraver of glass in the Stourbridge District in England, also worked in etching cased glass articles in the French style of cameo glass. He designed and executed many such pieces for Thomas Webb & Sons about the beginning of the 20th century. Kny's style differs greatly from the Continental cameo glass in color composition and design. When Kny's pieces are found, they are more likely to bear the Webb trademark or name than his own signature, since he is known to have signed very few of his works.

LOETZ OF AUSTRIA

In the heyday of l'art nouveau Loetz of Austria produced a few cameo pieces of real distinction, although he was primarily known for his iridescent glassware which he made contemporary to Tiffany's similar wares.

RUSSIAN CAMEO GLASS

The overlaid and decorated vase, pictured here as an example of Russian cameo glass, was obviously inspired by the Galle group of French glass artists. For a time its attribution presented a problem until the monogram on the base was identified as that of Czar Nicholas II, the last of the Romanov dynasty; dated 1909.

Threaded Glassware

by ALBERT CHRISTIAN REVI

***FIG. 1. Ancient glass vases with threaded designs, Greek, IV-VI centuries B.C.* Metropolitan Museum of Art.**

THE ART OF decorating glassware with applied glass threads, so widely practiced in the 19th century both in America and abroad, derived from an ancient Egyptian technique.

Early glassworkers of the Nile Valley decorated their glass objects by winding them with vari-colored threads of glass which they "combed" into feather-like patterns with a tool similar in appearance to a buttonhook. The designs made by the threads of glass were warmed into the surface of the article and smoothed out by rolling the object on a marver.

After the advent of blown glass in the 1st century A. D. when glass articles came into wider use, threads of glass were wound about objects for a practical purpose—to enable greasy hands to gain a better grip. Decorative aspects were not overlooked, however, for often these applied threads were of a contrasting color to the body glass.

Until the mid-nineteenth century, glass threads were applied by hand. The worker simply took up on a punty a gather of glass of any desired color. A slight touch of the gather to the body of the article was enough to start the process. The plastic metal adhered to the body of the article at the point of contact and the worker then began to rotate the article away from the punty, thus drawing the gather into a thread of glass which he applied to the neck or body of the article.

Then in 1876, William J. Hodgetts of the firm of Hodgetts, Richardson & Sons, Wordsley, England, patented a mechanical apparatus for applying glass threads to glass articles. It was first registered in England on May 6, 1876, and on November 26, 1878, Letters Patent were issued to Mr. Hodgetts in America.

FIG. 2. Machine threaded bowl and creamer, white threads on cranberry ground, ca. 1880.

This glass threading machine consisted of a mechanism for sustaining and revolving a glass bulb or cylinder in proximity to a gather of heated glass from which threads were to be drawn, at the same time causing the bulb and the thread-yielding gather to move past each other in the direction of the length of the bulb or cylinder. Through an ingenious use of two kinds of half screw-boxes, the motion of the bulb could be directed either forward or backward past the thread-yielding gather, thus applying a second coil of thread about the bulb or cylinder. In this way the threads could be made to overlap each other (in *Fig. 4,* the epergne on the extreme right is so threaded) or they could be made to wind in parallel with the first coil of threads.

Mr. Hodgetts suggested that window panes and door panels could be made from glass cylinders so decorated with vari-colored glass threads. Cylinders, after threading, could be split and flattened into sheets.

Another means for producing decorative effects with threaded glass was to pattern-mold the body glass in Venetian Diamond or other design prior to threading it. Often the body glass and the threads were of contrasting colors. The shimmering effects produced were striking. (See *Fig. 3.*) Applied raspberry prunts and rigaree decoration were often added to such pieces, especially those produced in England and on the Continent. The sophistication of the European designs is a telling factor in determining their origin.

FIG. 3. Lemonade glass with applied pink glass threads, engraved design of pond lilies and grasses, possibly Sandwich, 1880.

Mr. Hodgetts' machine was patented in several countries; however, with little alteration in the design this apparatus could be duplicated and still not infringe on his patent rights. Such a machine was patented December 8, 1877, by William Henry Stevens of Wordsley, near Stourbridge, England. The main functions of the Hodgetts' threading machine were duplicated in Mr. Stevens' patented design, although the apparatus itself was a little different. Later, on September 10, 1880, William Henry Stuart of Stafford, England, patented still another means of producing decorative threaded glassware. Mr. Stuart's idea included rolling the plastic parison in pulverized glass or enamel prior to threading the bulb. Reheating would cause the finely pulverized glass or enamel to melt and run while the glass threads remained intact and in place on the bulb.

In the *Pottery Gazette* for February, 1877, one writer mentions the "Allassantes" or "Sidonian" glass patented by a member of the Webb's firm. In such wares, colored threads of glass were attached to glass articles and the expansion caused by heat developed these threads into very curious but pleasing designs. The writer was no doubt referring to

***FIG. 4.** Two threaded glass epergnes and threaded candlestick, English, 1880.*
Brierley Hill Council House Collection.

FIG. 5. Large threaded glass footed bowl; body glass is pale pink with applied canary colored threads of glass; body of bowl pattern-molded with Venetian Diamond design. Collection of Mr. and Mrs. Ned Stinnett.

FIG. 6. Threaded deep rose pearlware vase, ca. 1880.

FIG. 7. "Tapestry" vase by Erard, 1892; threaded glass body with enamel decoration. Messrs. Stevens & Williams Ltd.

a patented method for ornamenting glassware taken out by Thomas Wilkes Webb, June 9, 1876. The decoration was haphazard in appearance and instead of showing well defined motifs produced with threads of glass, it consisted of random designs of colored trailings of glass, giving the impression of an ancient type glassware. A somewhat similar write-up was found in an American trade journal of the same year.

On February 20, 1885, John Northwood, the engraver of the first cameo glass reproduction of the Portland Vase, patented a machine for producing threaded glassware which did away with even more of the handwork still entailed, and tended to make the threading more uniform. Excerpts from his specifications accompany this text.

Marvering and the "warming in"

process caused the threads to sink into the body metal giving the article a smooth surface; even so, a careful study of wares made under Northwood's patent will reveal a slightly raised touch on the threaded portions. All such pieces examined by the writer have been marked "Patent" in the base with glossy letters; the rest of the article being acidized to a satin finish. The shell dish and the small vase in *Figs. 9 and 10* are examples of Mr. Northwood's patented method for producing this decorative effect.

Several pieces of this ware are exhibited at the Brierley Hill Council House from the collection of the inventor's son, John Northwood II. This ware has frequently been considered an American product and attributed to the Mt. Washington Glass Works. It is important, in the light of the foregoing, that such erroneous attributions be corrected.

Stevens & Williams of Brierley Hill carried threaded glassware another step forward by painting the threaded body with enamels. Erard was the artist most prominently associated with this "Tapestry" ware which was made at Stevens & Williams about 1892. (See *Fig. 7.*) Soon afterwards it was copied by the Bohemian factories.

Occasionally filigree glassware and pearlware (Mother - of - pearl Satin Glass) were further embellished by adding threads of glass to the body of the article. The pitcher shown in *Fig. 8* and the vase in *Fig. 6* are wonderful (and difficult to acquire) examples of such techniques.

European and American factories were quick to adopt machine threading for their wares. Its obvious advantages of uniformity and facility could not be overlooked. In an interview with Leslie Nash, son of Arthur Nash, the motivating genius in the

FIG. 8. Threaded filigree glass pitcher, 1880. **Collection Mrs. K's Toll House.**

FIG. 9. Threaded glass shell-shaped dish by John Northwood's patented process.

Fig. 10. Threaded glass vase by John Northwood's patented process. Collection of Mrs. Robert Neiman.

Tiffany glass factory, I learned that his father brought with him from England a machine for applying glass threads to glass articles. The use of such machinery had become so wide a practice that almost every glass-house of any real size had one in its shop. Each factory would add some modification to suit its special needs.

At the Sandwich Historical Society's museum on Cape Cod there are exhibited several pieces of threaded glass. Tall handled lemonade glasses, such as that shown in *Fig. 3,* cologne bottles, punch cups, and pitchers predominate but there are a few other articles, all rather loosely attributed to this venerable factory and thought by too many to be the singular work of Nicholas Lutz. It is true that fragments of machine threaded glass were unearthed at the old factory site and this does establish the production of such wares at Sandwich, but there is not enough evidence to warrant the positive attribution of all the pieces shown.

It is well to remember that fine examples of threaded glassware were made in considerable quantity by almost every important glass factory in England as well as in the United States, and that definite attribution is often extremely difficult, if not impossible.

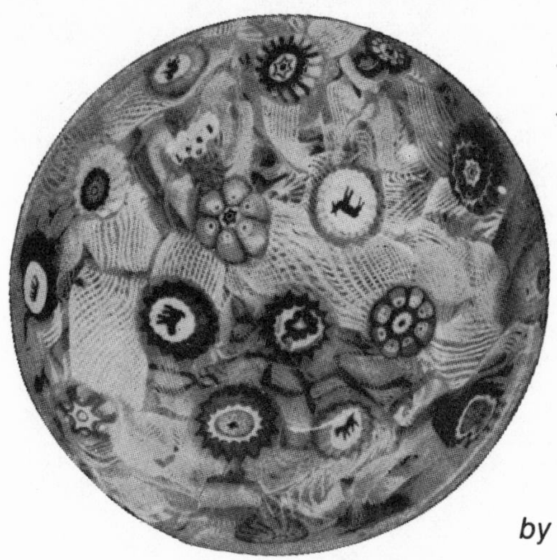

Signed and dated Baccarat paperweight with millefiori set-ups and filigree background.

Millefiori, Filigree and Striped Glass

by ALBERT CHRISTIAN REVI

THE story of the Venetian influence in the manufacture of 19th century glass actually goes back to ancient Egypt during the time of the Roman occupation and earlier, when the Egyptians were producing glass articles composed of what we now term "millefiori" rods. Deming Jarves, in his *Reminiscence of Glass-Making* (New York 1865), tells of ancient Egyptian glassware that contained "mosaic similar to the modern paperweight." The geographer Strabo relates that an Egyptian priest presented the Emperor Hadrian with several glass cups in mosaic, sparkling with every color, and deemed of such rare value that they were used only on great festivals.

The method of producing millefiori, or "mosaic rods" as Mr. Jarves termed them, was brought to the Roman Peninsula by Alexandrian craftsmen about 30 B.C. Hereby a bundle of variously colored glass rods was so arranged that its end resembled a rosette or mosaic. Bound tightly with reeds and subjected to intense heat, this bundle of multi-colored rods was fused into one rod which could, while in a plastic state, be pulled to any length and still retain its original pattern. In the 15th and 16th centuries, the Venetians developed the more elaborate rods used in the mid-19th century.

Some of the more intricate rods were produced in this way: molten

Striped glass ewer, American, ca. 1880.

Rare filigree glass tray, English, ca. 1880.

glass was poured into a pattern mold (often in the shape of animals, dancing figures, butterflies, stars, etc.) to form the core, or central motif of the finished rod. The patterned core, taken up on a punty, was dipped several times into a pot of fluid glass of contrasting color until it was well coated. Rolling the rod on a marver, the glass worker made it into a well shaped cylinder which could be pulled to a great length, and still retain its original pattern in miniature. Successive coatings of different colored metals, plus additional pattern-molding, made for more elaborate designs in the finished rod.

In 1848–1850, Jacopo Franchini, a glassblower in Murano, Italy, succeeded in manufacturing rods whose cross-sections revealed exquisite miniatures of ladies, elegantly gowned, and gentlemen in elaborate uniforms, resplendent with military sashes and medals. Some specimens of Franchini's work shown in the Smithsonian Institution have three and four half-length portraits in a single rod whose diameter and circumference are not much larger than that of an ordinary lead pencil. Such artistry in glass has never been equalled.

The earliest millefiori articles were produced by slicing the rods either obliquely or straight across and placing the little cross-section disks side by side in a terra-cotta mold. The mold was subjected to heat in the furnace where the disks fused together at the edges. This crude method of production limited the utility and size of the articles that could be made from millefiori rods.

With the discovery of the ductility of glass, sometime during the first century A.D., millefiori articles were manufactured differently. Into a heated mold, lined with cross-section disks, a bulb of plastic glass was inserted and expanded by further blowing. The little cross-section disks became embedded in the plastic metal and could then be handled like any other blown glass. Irregularities in the surface of the finished product were ground down to a smooth finish.

Millefiori articles such as paperweights were made by arranging small section or "set-ups" of millefiori rods in an upright position on a bed of plastic glass. A conical shaped mold, put over the arrangement, was filled with crystal glass. A punty was attached to what was to be the underside of the weight and the whole was dipped into a pot of fluid metal where it acquired a heavy coating of crystal. Shaping and polishing followed and the article emerged to dazzle the layman with its intricacies.

The production of what is correctly termed "filigree glass" began about the 1st or 2nd century B.C. The ancients produced filigree rods by twisting two or more opaque colored rods of glass rope-fashion while in a plastic state and subjecting them to extreme heat to fuse the rods together. These early rods were limited in use by the Venetians. Here, a bulb of plastic glass was blown into a heated mold, lined with colored or white rods alternated with crystal rods, and when withdrawn the colored and crystal rods adhered to its outer surface. Just as a drop of water added to a cupful will not be discernible from the whole, so the crystal rods when placed on the body of the crystal glass lose their individuality and only the colored rods are seen by the eye. By deftly twisting the inflated parison while it was still in a plastic state, the worker obtained the effect of colored and opaque threads spiralling around the body of the finished article.

Filigree glass goblet, applied dragon on knop stem, Venice, ca. 1875.

Ancient millefiori bowl shown courtesy the Metropolitan Museum of Art (New York).

The Venetian techniques of glass manufacture were imitated by the Bohemian, French, and English glass factories in the mid-19th century. The Bohemian factories of Neuwelt and Josephinenhutte produced some very fine millefiori and filigree wares. Gustave Pazaurek illustrated several superb examples in *Glaser der Empire und Beidermeierzeit.* The glasshouses of St. Louis, Clichy and Baccarat in France manufactured some of the finest examples of millefiori in a multitude of intricate paperweights and decorative articles. The production of filigree and striped glass articles also reached a high degree of craftsmanship in the capable hands of the French glass workers.

In England, the Venetian techniques did not become widely used until the last quarter of the 19th century. Prior to this, a few paperweights and some decorative articles made of millefiori and filigree rods had comprised the smallest segment of their output. Some excellent specimens of these wares were in evidence at the 1951 Exhibition of Glass at Stourbridge, England. The pieces shown were credited to the mid-19th century, about 1840–1845. Several drinking glasses, the stems of which were formed from filigree rods, were attributed to the 18th century. In 1887, Stevens & Williams of Brierley Hill, England, successfully produced and marketed glass articles which they termed "Venetian Filigree." Mr. Williams-Thomas, director of this firm, told me that the output was not great as the cost of production was, of necessity, very high.

The production of glass articles utilizing millefiori and filigree rods did not come to America until shortly after 1850. In 1860, Christian Dorflinger of White Mills, Pennsylvania, invited a large group of glassworkers from the St. Louis district of France to come to work for him in America. Among them was Nicholas Lutz.

It is, to all intents and purposes, impossible to distinguish articles of glass made by Nicholas Lutz from those produced by other capable glassmen. Though it has been claimed that certain types of applied crystal

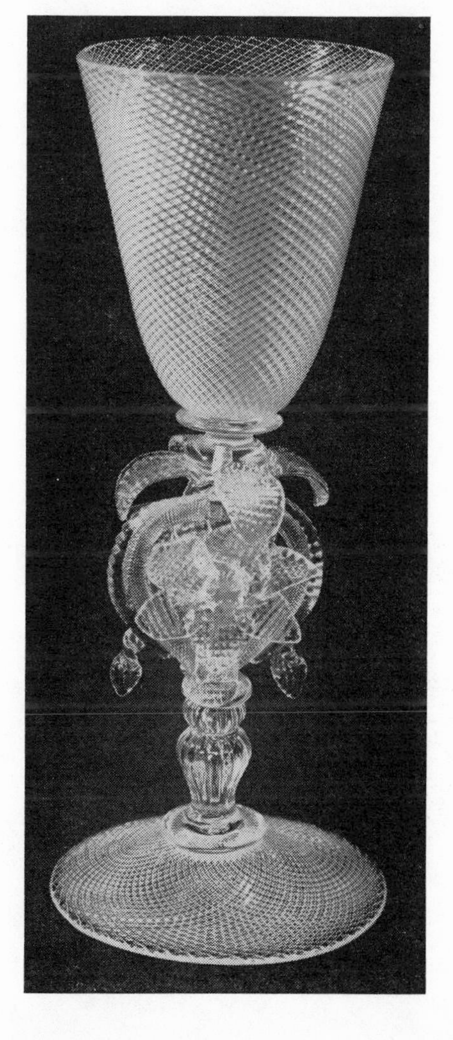

Above: Baccarat goblet with shadow-foliage engraving and selected florettes (Millefiori) in just the right places; cut blue and white filigree stem. **Right:** 16th century Venetian goblet, Latticinio or Vitro di Trina with air-traps. Corning Museum of Glass.

prunts on filigree, striped and threaded glassware positively identify the maker as Lutz, the fact is that similar decorative prunts were in use hundreds of years before the Christian era. Applied prunts were one of the earliest means of glass embellishment.

In the 19th century, labor was an expensive factor in the economy of the American glass factories; consequently the cost of producing millefiori and filigree rods was high. Some enterprising German importers located on West Broadway in New York City imported millefiori and filigree rods from Italy at a price which allowed their resale to glass factories in the United States at a cost much less than production cost here. Advertisements appeared in the trade catalogues at that time advising manufacturers of the availability of millefiori and filigree rods as well as rods of colored glass and rods of aventurine, at a "right" price. A controversy will always arise whenever a correct attribution of the wares manufactured from these imported rods is attempted.

Lalique's Madonna's and representations of the Saints are of a high order of ecclesiastic art. Photo Jean Collas, Paris.

In jewelry, R. Lalique designed pendants, corsage pins, highly styled hair combs, etc. Shown above is one of his collar ornaments.

René Lalique, Artist and Industrialist

by ALBERT CHRISTIAN REVI

THOUGH that stern critic John Ruskin rather harshly pronounced that the mechanical age had reduced the workers to a status of "cogs and compasses," there are still some who believe that a work of art must be unique in the true sense of the word before it has a reason for existence. It is to such artists that the masses, hungering for the diversion that beauty gives, turn for fulfillment. One man who devoted his life to just such artistic principles was René Lalique.

René Lalique was born in the little village of Ay, in the province of Champagne, in 1865. When he was two years old, his family moved to Paris, and it was there René received his education in the Ecole Turgot and in Fontenay-sous-Bois. During his formative years it was evident that he had a remarkable talent for original designs. At twenty, he was apprenticed to a jewelry firm where his artistic productions won him first prize for drawing and sculpture. His individual designs and his work with plastics soon brought him to the attention of Petitfils, Paris jewelers of note, for whom he executed special orders and designs for their selective clientele.

Later he joined the firm of Chez de Stape, then leading fashion jewelists of the world, at their workshop in Place Gallion, Paris. Here he experimented with enamels, instead of the customary rare metals, as a background for precious stones, achieving effects which revolutionized the jewelry trade. In each article of jewelry Lalique designed, the personality of the wearer was taken into consideration to make it an individual and distinctive production.

At thirty, he broke away from Chez de Stape to become a free-lance designer. In his studio at 3 Rue Therese

Fountain of architectural glass by Lalique at The Rond Point in Paris is well-known to thousands of visitors.

he modelled superb mountings for such jewelers as Cartier and Boucheron, and for the world famous actress, Sarah Bernhardt. In 1890, his first exhibition as an independent jeweler in the Salon des Artistes Francais won tremendous acclaim and brought royalty to his door for his personalized designs. From 1890 to 1904 he worked alone, creating all his designs and executing them himself in every detail.

At his new shop, 24 Place Vendome, he experimented with new ideas for mounting precious stones. He turned from the semi-precious tortoise-shell to ordinary horn because the former was too irregular in its coloring and offended his artistic tastes. This innovation met with immediate acceptance and as a result horn became a luxury in Paris. It was during his experiments with rock crystal that the idea of glass as a medium for expressing his artistic talents came to the fore and Lalique was headed down another road—a road which was to make him far more world renowned than he could ever have envisioned.

Glass was no strange substance to Lalique for he had used it in one form before, enamels — glass transformed with oxides. Scientifically he knew the ingredients for glass — sand, potash, lead. He understood the metal and recognized its tremendous possibilities in the hands of a master craftsman. In his own kitchen he made his first experiments, producing a tiny tear bottle. The bottle was molded in a simple cooking pan over the fire in his stove in the Rue Therese. In his eagerness to build up the intense heat needed for his experiments, he failed to recognize the obvious hazards and once while still deeply engrossed in his work, he suddenly became aware of crackling timber—his studio was afire. His first thought was for his experiment which he saved, while his landlord, rushing in, put out the fire. Consequently his landlord insisted he find other quarters.

Lalique decided he must have a laboratory of his own in which to carry on his work and also a shop to display it in. He decided to build to his own specifications at 40 Cour Albert Ier, thus adding architecture as another facet to his already full life. Lalique supervised every detail of the building of his new salon, still world famous for its beauty. The door of sculptured glass was his first architectural glass design.

When approached by the perfumer Coty to design a label for his product, Lalique designed instead a whole new bottle, a triumph in artistic glass. The bottle and the perfume made both men famous.

In 1920 René Lalique acquired his present glassworks at Wingen-sur-Moder in Alsace-Lorraine. Here he produced on a large scale artistic glass designs, of which representative pieces can be found in almost every museum in the world.

For the most part Lalique glassware is molded or cast in a mold. Sometimes Lalique combined cutting with casting, obtaining some rather pleasing effects. Certain areas of the molded designs were treated with acids to produce a frosted or gelid effect on the glass, often in combina-

Exquisite boudoir pieces by Lalique are well balanced and functional; stoppers with cascading blooms show exceptionally delicate design.

tion with bright glistening surfaces which were either cut and polished, treated with acids to give bright effects, or simply left in the original state as it came from the mold after fire polishing.

His blown wares were almost all confined to cups of glass, stemware, and large bottles, but even in these instances the stem and foot of the glass and the neck of the bottle were molded.

Another method of manufucture, not often encountered by collectors, were those pieces made by the *Cire Perdue,* or "lost wax," method. These were unique designs first modelled in wax, then covered with a ceramic paste. After the paste had hardened, the paste-covered model was placed in an oven to melt out the wax model, leaving a hollow ceramic mold. Into this ceramic mold was poured molten glass. The mold was broken away after the glass had annealed leaving a perfect reproduction of the wax model in glass.

For color, Lalique depended on

A copy of this horsehead from the original design of René Lalique is prominently displayed in the foyer of Lalique's Paris Studios. Photo Jean Coquin, Paris.

transluced glass, opaline, or colored glass—black, smoked, jade green, sapphire blue or red. On occasion irisated effects were produced on the surface of the glass by subjecting it to gaseous fumes in a muffle. Colored enamels, transparent and opaque, were utilized with beautiful results.

It was originally intended that each piece of glass that left the Lalique factory be marked "Lalique," and as far as possible such was the case. However, the human element cannot always be governed and it is understandable that some pieces have left the works without any identifying marks. Comparison with signed pieces will tell the owner whether or not he has an unmarked Lalique creation.

Lalique's productions cover an almost infinite range, from tableware to architectural glass. Stemware, tumblers, pitchers, carafes, trays, ice buckets, plates, bowls, and dessert sets of all kinds have a beauty of line and color seldom found in such every day household articles. Each piece is well balanced and functional. Boudoir accessories were given particular attention. A wide variety of beautiful perfume and cologne bottles have been manufactured. Each design has a personality all its own, from the light whimsical air of nymphs and mimosa blossoms cascading in delicate sprays from the stopper of the bottle to the heady beauty of large full-blown flowers rising from the top of the decanter like some exquisite nosegay. Dresser trays, powder and ointment jars, jewel boxes and many other articles to grace a lady's boudoir are superbly expressed in glass by Lalique.

For the house proper, René Lalique designed hundreds of beautiful accoutrements from tiny press-molded figurines and vases three or four inches high to extremely large pieces eighteen or twenty inches tall. Decorative lighting fixtures were also made. Some indescribably beautiful effects were produced by indirect lighting, such as the fantastic battle of the Knights of the Sea astride their grotesque horses; or the superb grouping of peacocks with their feathery tails spread out in glorious profusion. Chandeliers and lamps capable of producing not only illumination but also a decorative function when in repose were manufactured. Clocks, ashtrays, covered boxes, medallions, and a host of other useful household articles were given his customary touch of elegance.

Architectural glass is perhaps one of his most important contributions to interior and exterior decoration. No longer was there a need to cover with brick and mortar when beautifully molded glass could be utilized to add light and dignity to otherwise dark and dismal areas. Doors, corrugated walls, gates, mantels, balustrades, wainscoting, windows, fountains, and pavilions all glowed with that soft illumination only glass can impart.

Lalique's use of architectural glass in churches and shrines was his contribution to the Divine. His complete altars, crucifixes, Madonnas and representations of Saints will take their place in the annuals of ecclesiastic art beside the superb stained glass windows of the 14th and 15th centuries. Beholding all these worthy achievements in glass one is struck by the fact that each article is a true representation of functional beauty.

Few men are blessed with a son who shares his father's enthusiasm and artistic abilities. In Marc Lalique, René had a rare companionship, and a son's fulfillment of all his paternal needs and expectations. Marc's early training with his father fitted him for the future handling of the business along his father's idealistic, yet practical, lines. Present day productions under Marc Lalique could not be finer were they still under the loving aegis of his father-teacher.

With the same awareness of the needs of this generation that his father had shown for those of the past generation, plus newer and better methods of production, Marc Lalique has made available to the public a greater number of beautiful objects at a much reduced cost. This practice would have completely pleased his famous father whose sincere desire it had always been to bring mankind beautiful objects in glass at a price all could afford.

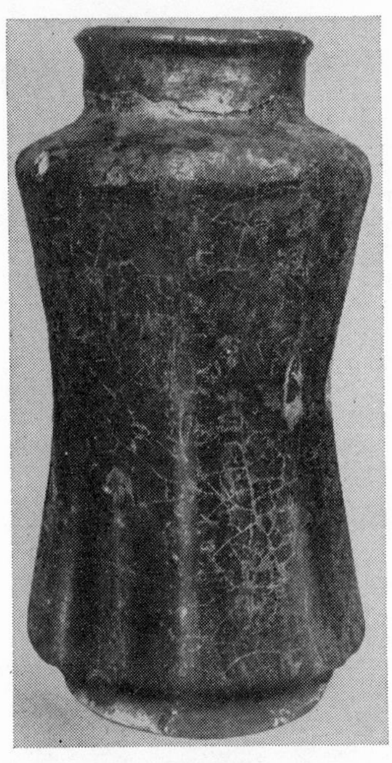

13th century albarello, 7" high, from Rakka, Mesopotamia, shows greenish-blue glaze beneath golden iridescence. (Smithsonian Institution)

Iridescent Glass Through the Ages

by ALBERT CHRISTIAN REVI

Surface shimmering with rainbow hues,
Purple and crimson and turquoise blues,
Ruby and orange, yellow and green;
Each of them decked in glorious sheen.
—Abraham Lomax in *Royal Lancastrian Pottery*

IRIDESCENCE on glass is caused by the action of carbonic acid or ammonia salts contained in the air or the earth which, in the presence of moisture, decomposes the glass, forming soluble carbonate of soda or potash. As this is washed from the surface of the glass, there remain small scales of an acid silicate of lime, alumina, or lead, as the case may be, which breaks up the rays of the light, giving the iridescent effect.

Iridescence occurs when glass lies buried in humid earth at high temperatures; it is also found on glass objects taken from Roman, Egyptian, and Grecian tombs. Once the conditions are met, deterioration or decomposition of the glass can begin in a comparatively short time. This is evidenced by the iridescent film one finds on bits of glass exposed to the elements along roadsides and highways.

In *5000 Years of Glass-making,* J. R. Vavra suggests that ancient glassmakers frequently iridized glass:

"The Romans knew how to give glass a metal sheen. It was not identical with that found in old glasses after they had been buried in the earth for hundreds of years. . . . The Romans added a certain resin to the salts and made their glasses iridescent 'golden' by the use of silver, and 'blue' by the use of bismuth. Franchet asserts that he gained similar results with Roman recipes."

While Mr. Vavra's information would seem to establish that glass was artificially iridized at a very early date, his premises are not wholly accepted by all experts in the field of ancient glass.

It has been generally considered that what the modern glassmaker sought in iridizing glass was to produce on the surface an exceedingly thin metallic film. This cannot be entirely true, for such a film of some metals, i.e., platinum, is not iridescent. Rather, the glassmaker sought to produce a finely ridged metallic film that would split ordinary daylight into its constituent colors. Ordinary daylight, or white light, becomes separated when light is bent or refracted as, for instance, in a thin layer of oil on the surface of water. It is this assemblage of many colors that produces iridescence.

The development of modern methods of producing iridescent effects on glass and pottery can best be traced through a review of the processes registered in various countries abroad.

March 9, 1877, Louis Clemandot, civil engineer of Paris, France, registered a process for producing iridescence by employing, under pressure of 2 to 5 or 6 atmospheres, water acidulated with hydrochloric acid in the proportion of 15% of acid. This resulted in nacreous and iridescent effects analogous to those produced by time and atmospheric agents on antique glass.

August 29, 1877, Thomas Wilkes Webb of Thos. Webb & Sons, Stourbridge, England, registered a process calling for the use of a closed muffle or chamber wherein fumes from the evaporation of tin and other metallic salts were made to play directly upon the surface of glasses enclosed in this chamber. The acid involved, having an affinity to the molten surface of the glass, remained permanently attached thereto, thus producing rainbow or prismatic tints upon the surface of the glass. On October 12, 1878, an addition was made to this process and registered under another patent. It explained the manufacture of crackled iridescent glassware which Thos. Webb & Sons produced. The article was immersed several times during the making into a vat of water, thus adding a fine crackled effect to the iridescent lustre.

November 29, 1877, Sidney Wittman, an "importer of goods of all types," Great Marlborough St., London, was granted only provisional protection for his method for iridizing glass surfaces, whereby the glass was boiled in a solution of muriatic acid under pressure of several atmospheres. The iridized material was used primarily as inlay in ornamental furniture, such as ebony and other fancy woods, probably in imitation of Chinese furniture inlaid with mother-of-pearl shell. Nevertheless, it could be applied to hollow wares of all kinds.

November 29, 1878, Messrs. Monot, pere et fils, and Stumpf, of Paris, France, were issued two patents covering processes for metallizing and iridizing glassware. The metallic oxides in the glass itself were subjected to a reducing flame which produced a metallized or bronzed effect on the surface of the glass. Specifically mentioned was oxide of copper, which the first patent states will produce this bronzed or golden sheen on glass. The second patent dealt primarily with a crackling effect produced on the glass much the same as that mentioned in Webb's specifications.

July 4, 1881, T. D. McDermot of Surrey, England, was issued a patent for producing an iridescent effect by subjecting the article to carbonic acid fumes. This did not form a true iridescence, but instead, resembled the metallic film used on mirror backs.

December 21, 1881, Rice W. Harris, of Calais, France, was granted a patent for a process which achieved an effect similar to McDermot's. This also employed carbonic acid fumes but in connection with some other unmentioned metallic chlorides.

Patera, cup or bowl, 1st century A.D., of thin glass, blue tinted, with iridescent crustation, 2¾" high, diameter at rim 2 11/16". (Corning Museum of Glass)

October 5, 1889, Franz Emil Grosse, of Berlin, Germany, was issued a patent for producing an iridizing effect on rolled, blown, or pressed window glass and hollow wares. The glass was subjected to the fumes of pink salts, or the salts were sprinkled on the surface of the glass before it was placed in the annealing ovens. The oxidized salts would then produce a metallic iridescent sheen on the glass.

February 27, 1892, John Jacobson of Boston, Mass., was issued an English patent for a quite different iridizing process. He pressed his glass in molds to impart an extremely fine corrugated effect on the glass object. His process seems to have been confined to buttons and flat sheets of glass. The lines formed on the facets of artificial gems and buttons numbered not less than three thousand to the inch. The idea was probably taken from the observance that iridescence in mother-of-pearl shells was obtained by fine laminae or scales on the surface of the shell.

The two patents issued to Frederick S. Shirley, Mt. Washington Glass Works, New Bedford, Massachusetts, on August 13, 1878, though pointed to the same end, were entirely different in their elements and methods of working. An American trade journal for October 31, 1878, writing of the "Rainbow or Iris Glassware" being produced by the Mt. Washington works, described these processes:

"In one . . . the article is submitted to a degree of heat sufficient not only to insure freedom from moisture but also to expand the surface, rendering it susceptible to absorbing vapors or gases in which it may be enveloped; these gases being produced by the vaporizing of mixtures of Iodide or Bromine or solutions of them or their equivalents in alcohol, petroleum, etc. By these means, articles which have in themselves little or no color acquire a surface tint with every variety of color and shade from the lightest silver yellow to the deepest wine color . . . the depth of color being dependent on the time the article may be exposed in the muffle or oven and the amount of impregnating material absorbed by it.

"By another method the articles are taken while still in the course of manufacture and submitted to the action of a gaseous vapor which acts on the surface of the material exposed to it; this, however, must be done at the precise moment when the gas contains the correct proportion of free acid, which is instrumental in depositing the tinted coating. . . . This is done by heating a closed receptacle having a slide door or some ready means of closing and inserting the article at the requisite heat and filling the chamber with gas. Though this method is by far the most certain, and greater brilliancy is obtained, the greatly increased expense in operating renders it less desirable for common use than that by which the article is exposed to the gaseous vapor as directly produced from the compound."

Contemporary writers and most all patent specifications omit certain pertinent elements necessary to the manufacture of colored iridescent glassware. The most important omission is mention of the decided degree to which tints produced on the glass are influenced by the color of the body glass.

For instance, Tiffany's iridescent "Mohammedan blue," known to collectors as "butterfly blue" depended greatly for its color on the fact that the body glass was a deep cobalt blue. The famous "peacock" iridescent colors for which this firm became famous were all produced on translucent glasses of a dark blue, green, or red color. The light golden iridescent pieces had a body glass of a translucent pale amber color.

Opaque white and colored glasses did not lend themselves well to refracting the scintillating highlights produced by the iridizing agents, and were used sparingly.

Threads of different colored glass were applied to the body of the article and "combed" into intricate designs before the article was subjected to the coruscating fumes of the metallic salts. The different colored glasses resulted in varied hues in the iridescent effects produced. The changeable iridescent blue, red, and green highlights produced on some wares were the result of a change in the color of the iridescent film brought about by the heat of the muffle

Cameo effects, applied prunts, and even florettes from millefiori rods used on early iridescent pieces, were applied to the body of the article for decorative effect.

In the Crockery & Glass Journal, dated January 9, 1875, mention was made of an iridescent glass tumbler manufactured in Hungary and bought there by a Mr. N. M. Lowe of Boston, Massachusetts, for two florins (about $1 U. S. money at that time). The iridescence was due to a surface treatment which was supposed to be a closely guarded secret, but as Mr. Lowe commented, "It could be had in America."

Charles K. Ovington, in the winter of 1878, reported on iridescent glass in an American trade journal:

"Modern chemists and glassmakers have long been trying to discover the art of making glass iridescent by some more speedy means than that of burying it in a damp soil for the benefit of a thankless posterity. With all the progress made in kindred branches of the art, nothing of note was done in this direction until two French chemists quite recently succeeded in artificially producing this iridescence.

"The process they made use of [Louis Clemandot's patent, Paris, 1877] is said to consist essentially in submitting the glass under a considerable pressure and at an elevated temperature to the action of water containing fifteen percent of hydrochloric acid. Only certain kinds of glass are suitable for this operation. The action of this acid is thought to be analogous to that of the elements upon older glass in dissolving the alkaline silicates and leaving the surface of the glass finely ridged or corrugated, and thus capable of refracting the light with prismatic or rainbow colors like those of mother-of-pearl.

"Peligot, the celebrated French chemist, speaking of ancient glass says, 'The iridescence is caused by fine scales or laminae which may be removed by gentle rubbing.' The modern glass stands any amount of rubbing or cleaning without losing this curious property; but if the exposed surface be cut or ground off, the iridescent effect is instantly lost, showing that its cause is merely superficial and not structural.

"The Bohemian glass so far seems to be the favourite for embellishing with the new iridescence. Bohemian glass will resist a much greater heat than any other kind, and it is made in graceful shapes and is clear and transparent. At present, the leading Bohemian factory [Lobmeyer's Works at Zlatno, Hungary] is producing a good deal of this iridescent glassware, principally for the European market, as the American public is hardly as yet acquainted with this novel and beautiful glassware. . . .

"As to the articles of glassware to which this enrichment may be applied, there seems to be almost no limit. . . . Large crystal balls, highly iridescent, and resembling soap-bubbles in everything but frailty, are very beautiful; the glasses intended to hold white and light colored wines give a piquant color to the contents by the sparkle of the rainbow hues upon the cup. But nothing has such charm as delicate crystal copies of old Roman and Cypriote glass urns and vases glistening with iridescent colors."

The following year in 1879, when C. F. A. Hinrichs, New York City, wholesale distributors, received from Bohemia "the finest selection of iridescent glass and bronze glass ever assembled under one roof," the Crockery & Glass Journal editorialized:

"In the Bronze glass the Pompeiian and antique styles prevail. These are interesting as well as beautiful, especially so as being exact copies of relics rescued from the ruins of the buried city. The iridescent glass goods are of the most perfect finish and graceful shapes and glitter in the light with all the hues of the rainbow. Here are vases and bouquet holders of unique forms, and of all sizes, mingled with more practical articles of tableware, such as goblets, finger-bowls, wines, etc. . . . Among the vases in iridescent glass are a number of elegant ones decorated with engraved and cameo work, with medallions rich with beautiful birds and flowers. The Bronze vases are also, many of them, finely ornamented. A superb line of bouquet-holders have the vase and base in iridescent, the body, representing a tulip, being in bronzed glass. The combination is in admirable taste, and the result strikingly rich. The iridescent crackle ware is another attractive novelty which must take with people of good taste."

An 1878 London trade journal carried a commentary by Her Majesty Queen Victoria:

"On a recent visit to Mr. Goode's attractive galleries at Audley Street we noticed a fine selection of the new Bronze glass, discovered and made by Messrs. Thos. Webb & Sons of Stourbridge. Its purple bronze surface shines with the hues of the rainbow, such as they appear on molten lead, or on pieces of steel which have been tempered in gradually diminishing degrees of heat. . . . The shapes are in preference borrowed from Dr. Schliemann's finds at Troy and Mycenae, owl-faced and curiously-lipped vessels predominating. . . . It has already attracted considerable attention at the Paris Exhibition (1878), likewise at the Grosvenor Gallery, where Mr. Goode placed some of his finest specimens."

An American trade journal of the same year commented on the growing popularity of iridescent ware, and the new results that were constantly being attained by carefully guarded experiments, rival manufacturers fearing lest others take advantage of

Iridescent tumbler, Bohemia, 1875.

their efforts in developing this ware.

"This seems to have been the case in regard to the production of Iris or Rainbow glassware," it reported, "for it appears that desultory efforts to obtain hues on glassware and similar substances (glazed pottery and tiles) have been simultaneously carried on by several parties in districts entirely remote from each other, as in France, Bohemia, and England, and also in this country. . . .

"The accidental production of these colors has been long known and often proved a serious annoyance to manufacturers, and was considered a detriment even to the articles themselves, occurring as it did in a haphazard way and not producible at will, while the colors generally lacked the intensity and brilliancy desired and produced in present manufacture."

(Sulphurous fumes from the furnace frequently escaped and formed a "sulphur bloom" on glassware, usually while the articles were being worked or shaped at the glory hole. These "blooms" were sometimes an iridescent discolorization.)

In the fall of 1878, the Mt. Washington Glass Works was advertising:

NEW HOLIDAY GOODS!

The NEW BRONZE GLASS, in all the Original Grotesque Forms, as discovered at Ancient Troy and Mycenae.

SOLE MANUFACTURERS OF THE NEW "RAINBOW" or "IRIDESCENT" GLASSWARE IN THE U.S.

N. B. The patent on this glass has been for a long time in interference and is now declared and issued giving the ENTIRE CONTROL of the manufacture and sale of these goods to this company. To meet the wants of the trade, we shall keep a large variety of styles in these goods, both of our own manufacture and imported.

A few months later, early in 1879, the Crockery & Glass Journal noted:

"We learn that the U. S. Patents controlling the manufacture and sale of iridescent glassware in this country have been just sold for $5,000.00; the present owner assuming all suits on the same, and looking for his return in the royalties to be collected on the manufacture."

In *Sandwich Glass,* Ruth Webb Lee included a letter from W. A. H. Schrieber, written from Philadelphia, May 12, 1878, to Mr. Fessenden of the Boston & Sandwich Glass Company proffering the rights to produce iridescent glassware in the United States, apparently the same rights which had been sold to Webb & Sons in England, to Salviati in Venice, and "two or three other parties in Bohemia and Germany."

From the editorial in the Crockery & Glass Journal, and the Mt. Washington Glass Work's advertisements, it would appear that the Sandwich Boston and Sandwich Company did not take up the rights Mr. Schreiber offered. This does not preclude the possibility that iridescent wares were manufactured at the Cape Cod works, but we would advise a cautious approach to this premise. We have no concrete evidence that iridescent glassware was produced at Sandwich.

A thorough search of the U. S. Patent files failed to turn up any other specifications for the manufacture of iridescent glassware than those issued to Mr. Shirley. It is obvious that he saw the possibilities in this iridescent glassware and negotiated the sale of the patent rights for his firm.

Contemporary magazines and trade journals fail to disclose just what firm or firms were contesting the Mt. Washington works for the rights to produce iridescent wares. The only indication we could find of any other American firm manufacturing iridescent glass at that period was in a description of Hobbs, Brockunier & Company's display at the Mechanics Fair in Boston, October 14, 1878, which noted: "The goods shown by this firm are displayed on a handsome table, and consist of blown, pressed, and etched ware in crystal and in colors, and *in iridescent glass.*" Although Hobbs, Brockunier ran full page and half-page advertisements in all of the trade journals constantly during this period, we failed to find mention of their iridescent glassware

Iridescent glass bowl, with "flecking" dispersed throughout the metal; Stevens & Williams, England, ca. 1890. Enamel and gilt decoration by E. Erard. Brierly Hill Library Collection.

in any of them. It is a probability that they were enjoined from producing and selling it because of some legal action taken by the Mt. Washington Glass Works.

Imported iridescent wares continued to be sold. Hinrichs & Company, in 1887, was advertising in trade papers a Bohemian iridescent glass called "Nacre de Perle"; there were occasional advertisements by Salviati & Cie, of Venice; and Stevens & Williams in England were putting out iridescent ware in limited scale.

Interest in iridescent glass which had flagged in the late 1880s and 1890s was revived in the early 1900s by American and Continental glasshouses. In France iridescent glass and pottery became one phase of design and manufacture of that short-lived renaissance known as *l'Art Nouveau.* In America, the most prominent manufacturers of iridescent glasses were Tiffany Furnaces, Steuben Glass Works, the Quezal Art Glass & Decorating Company, the Durand Art Glass Company and The Union Glass Works.

Tiffany Furnaces: After one abortive attempt to establish a glass works, Louis C. Tiffany engaged the services, on a share-holding basis, of Arthur J. Nash, formerly of England. Mr. Nash was joined by his sons, A. Douglas and Leslie. The elder Nash and Leslie operated the factory at Corona, Long Island, and were responsible for all the designs, glass formulas, and decorating techniques. Douglas Nash was the outside contact, in charge of the distribution of the factory's wares, dealing with better shops all over the country and abroad.

Several trademarks were registered by Tiffany between the years 1894 and 1920. The first was granted to the "Tiffany Glass and Decorating Company" located in Jersey City, New Jersey, and New York City. After February 9th, 1904, the company was known as "Tiffany Furnaces of Corona, Long Island, and Hoboken, New Jersey."

As early as 1894, the following terms of identification were used for its glassware: *Tiffany Favrile Fabric Glass, Tiffany Favrile Sunset Glass, Tiffany Favrile Horizon Glass, Tiffany Favrile Twig Glass,* and *Tif-*

Late iridescent pressed wares: marigold decanter in heavy grape design, blown stopper; low footed compote, satin finish, "deer and holly" pattern; "Pressed-cut" fruit bowl on separate standard.

fany Favrile Lace Glass. When Leslie Nash developed a method for making lamp shades by coating a copper mesh screen with glass, the trademark, *Favrile Fabrique,* was registered in June, 1914.

The Nashes, because of their superior development of iridescent and other fine wares, brought the Tiffany works to first place in the production of artistic glass in America. Contrary to many reports, we have been told by a reliable source that Mr. Tiffany had no practical experience in glassmaking and did not personally sign every piece which bore the Tiffany trademark or initials.

At first, the Nashes encountered tough sledding to make ends meet at the factory, but Leslie Nash developed several very useful artistic and commercial products that brought the company onto firm financial ground; this in spite of Mr. Tiffany's efforts to run the works on a philanthropic basis.

An accomplished glass technologist in his own right, he was awarded a partnership in the Tiffany Furnaces for his development of the world famous "Peacock" iridescent glass. Leslie also introduced the manufacture of fine metalwares like bronze, copper, and combinations of rare and semi-precious metals. He purchased huge metal stamping machinery to make the fine fittings for their glassware which distinguish many of the Tiffany productions. Mr. Tiffany's withdrawal of his financial support from the firm just at this most crucial period was a shock to the Nashes, especially so, when for the first time in years they were finally writing their ledgers in the black. For a while they carried on the business in the same fashion as under the old plans which had included Mr. Tiffany: Arthur Nash and Leslie ran the works while Douglas Nash continued to do the outside contracting. However after a short period of operation, the Nashes decided to close the factory.

Steuben Glass Works: "Aurene" was the registered trade name for the iridescent wares produced at the Steuben Glass Works of Corning, New York. It was granted Sept. 6th, 1904. Fred R. Carder signed the papers as Secretary of the firm, with Samuel Hawkes and W. H. Hawkes as witnesses. The two last named were both financially and actively connected with the firm at its inception.

In the course of our extensive research into the field of iridescent glassware, we were privileged to have several talks with Fred Carder, whose beautiful "Aurene" and "Verre de Soie" rank among the best iridescent glasses ever made in America. Mr. Carder spoke of Lobmeyer as being the first in his opinion to make iridescent glassware. Lobmeyer would introduce tin crystals into a muffle and the fumes from these oxidizing crystals attacked the surface of the glass subjected to them causing a corruscated effect. Mr. Carder produced the same effect by spraying the heated glass with a solution of tin crystals dissolved in water.

The idea of the Steuben Works being sued for patent infringement by Tiffany Furnaces, as has occasionally been mentioned, seems far-fetched, especially since neither of these firms ever registered patent specifications for iridizing glassware. Significantly, none of the other 20th century producers made any attempts at registering iridizing processes. Neither the Nashes nor Mr. Carder were the first to produce iridescent effects on glass, nor were they to be the last. The later introduction of cheap pressed iridescent glass was one of the primary reasons such fine wares were discontinued by the Corning and Corona Works.

Quezal: Blown iridescent glassware was made by the Quezal Art Glass & Decorating Company, located at Fresh Pond Road and Metropolitan Avenue, in Brooklyn, New York. Its founder, Martin Bach, was once a trusted employee at the Tiffany Furnaces, working directly under Mr. Arthur Nash. Leslie Nash told us that some of the techniques used at the Quezal factory were those practiced at the Corona plant.

In our own files we have the trademark paper filed by Mr. Bach for the name "Quezal" as applied to fancy glasswares. It is dated October 28, 1902 and signed by Martin Bach as president. The iridescent glasses produced by this firm are of a fine quality in both form and color.

Durand: The Durand Art Glass Company of Vineland, New Jersey, owned and operated by Victor Durand, was very ably occupied in producing beautiful iridescent glasswares, as well as other types of art glass. Pieces of his ware were signed with his monogram which consisted of the name "Durand" within a large "V," or simply marked in script "Durand." The Durand works operated contemporary with Tiffany Furnaces, Steuben, and Quezal.

Col. Ewan Kimball also operated a glass furnace in Vineland, New Jersey. We were unable to find any patent rights or trademark papers issued to either Kimball or Durand but this is not unusual since neither tradename could have been infringed on to advantage. At one time Messrs. Kimball and Durand are said to have operated jointly as "Kimball & Durand" but with little success.

Union Glass Company: The Union Glass Company of Somerville, Massachusetts made iridescent glassware and named it "Kew Blas." Their iridescent wares are also contemporary with Tiffany's. The name "Kew Blas" is said to be an anagram of the plant foreman's name (W. S. Blake) but is more likely derived instead from the words "keweeanawite," (an arsenide of copper, nickel and cobalt, the fumes of which were used in making iridescent glassware) and "blas," which Webster defines as "an emanation from the stars—coined by Van Helmont." The Union Glass Work's iridescent wares differ little from those manufactured by other firms and unless they are signed "Kew Blas," it would be almost impossible to distinguish them from other iridescent glasses made in the early part of the 20th century.

Loetz: A fine quality iridescent glassware was made in Austria by Loetz. The vase illustrated here was an obvious attempt at reproducing the beautiful Peacock iridescent glassware made by Tiffany Furnaces. Loetz of Austria was also noted for its fine cameo effects inspired by the French Cameo Glass of the *Art Nouveaux* era. (See *French Cameo Glass,* page 67.)

The Stourbridge District: While we were in England we spent a great deal of time talking with John Northwood, Jr. about the glass made in the Stourbridge district. Our talks embraced iridescent glassware and Mr. Northwood spoke of the extensive experiments he and his father carried on in this field shortly before the turn of the century. They learned that chloride of iron, in a low state of fusion, could be made to produce more colored iridescent effects than any of the other oxides.

Pressed Iridescent Wares: Mr. Northwood remembered, too, that some time after the turn of the century his brother Harry, who had long since left England to ply his trade in America, sent him a piece of pressed iridescent glass and asked him to analyze the surface coating for him. A rival company was manufacturing this pressed iridescent ware, Harry said, and unless he could learn to produce it himself he stood to lose considerably. After much tedious work, John Northwood finally isolated the material and determined that it was chloride of iron. A few months after he made his report to his brother, a shipment of Harry's pressed iridescent glass was delivered to him in England.

Prominent in the field of late pressed iridescent glassware were The Fenton Art Glass Works of Williamstown, West Virginia; The Imperial Glass Company of Belaire, Ohio; and, of course, the Northwood Company of Wheeling, West Virginia and Indiana, Pennsylvania.

Iridescent Pottery: Pottery with an iridescent glaze was also produced in this late period. The pitcher shown bears an original paper label identifying it as a Tiffany product. The Royal Lancastrian Potteries of Messrs. Pilkington of England stands out as probably the most artistic lustred or iridescent pottery of our time (1900-1938). In Germany, Zsolnay was the major producer of fine iridescent pottery.

INDEX TO ILLUSTRATIONS

Examples pictured, with exceptions noted, from author's collection.

(1) Brilliant Mazarin blue iridescent sheen on deep blue glazed pottery pitcher; body and handle forms are unique; original paper label identifies it as from Tiffany Studios.

(2) Iridescent gold, silver, and lavender vase, drag design in leaf pattern, signed "Quezal". (Collection Mrs. Claranell Lewis).

(3) Opaque white and red vase with iridescent gold and green drag decoration, made by Fred Carder of the Stueben Glass Works.

(4) "Verre de soie" wine glass, bowl flecked with mica, stem is green, made by Fred Carder, Steuben.

(5) Brilliant iridescent glass vase, drag design, signed "Corona", possibly an early Nash trademark.

(6) Iridescent glass vase, peacock feather drag loop design, signed "Loetz of Austria".

(7) Apricot colored vase with iridescent sheen, signed "Durand".

(8) Brilliant iridescent vase with drag design, signed "Louis C. Tiffany, Favrile".

(9) Brilliant iridescent glass vase in seashell form, expert craftsmanship and design, unmarked.

(10) Iridescent green glass vase decorated with lustrous striations, 9" high, ca. 1900, by J. Lotz' Witwe of Klostermuhle, Austria (Loetz of Austria). *Victoria & Albert Museum.*

(11) Iridescent gold and silver violet vase, millefiori florettes embedded in surface of glass, signed "Aurene".

(12) Decanter and stopper of green iridescent glass, marked "L.C.T.", ca. 1900, 11" high. *Victoria & Albert Museum.*

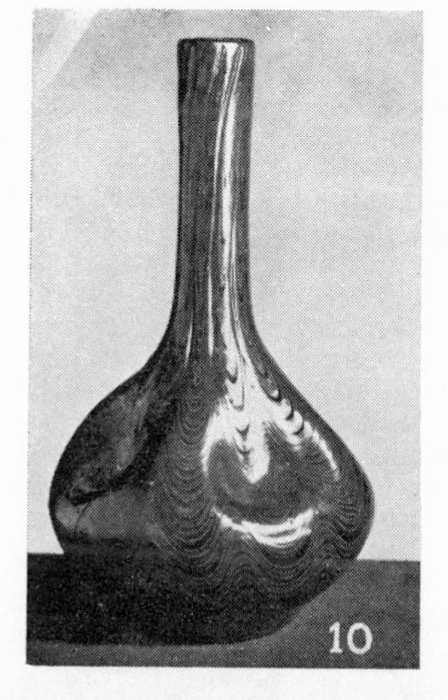
10

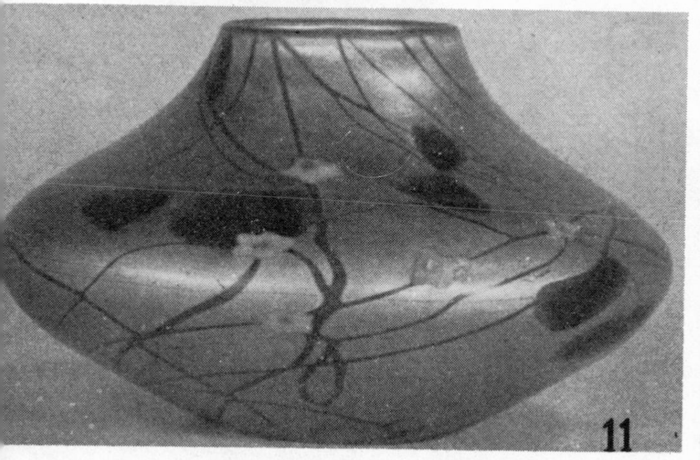
11

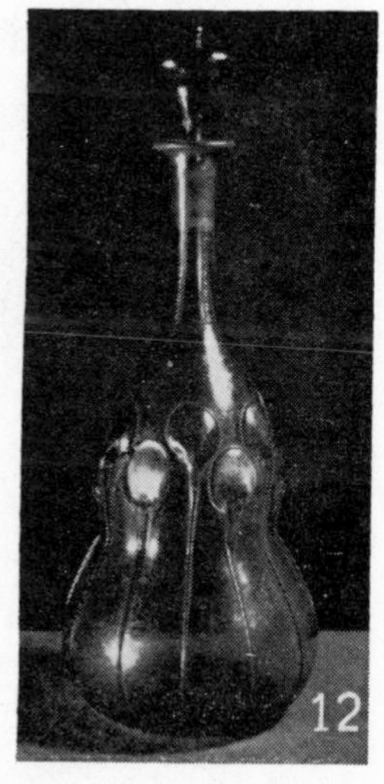
12

The Art Glass of Louis Comfort Tiffany

by J. JONATHAN JOSEPH

LOUIS COMFORT Tiffany was born in 1848, the son of Charles Tiffany, one of the founders of Tiffany & Co. From childhood he showed remarkable concern with color, and inevitably he turned to art rather than to his father's business.

Greatly influenced by the color work of George Inness, the American painter, young Louis began to study painting seriously at the age of eighteen. Born to great wealth, at a time when the Grand Tour of Europe was a "must," and consequent "drifting" was fashionable, he pursued his studies abroad with a passion and direction which amazed his masters. Painting in both oil and water color, he was at last able to translate his exotic feeling for color into something tangible. This quality is expressed strongly in his paintings of North Africa and Southern Europe.

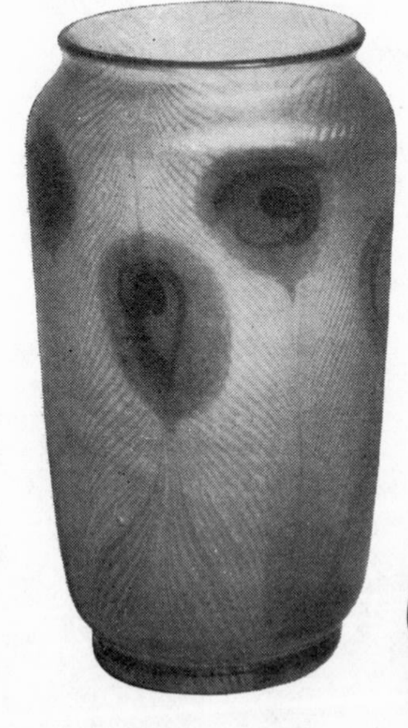

Left: Pale blue iridescent vase with famous "Peacock Eye" decoration, a very rare technique, not to be confused with the simpler feather decoration; "eyes" are deeper blue with black iridescent centers; 5¼" high; inscribed "L. C. Tiffany-Favrile No. V228. **Right:** Black iridescent miniature vase with blue iridescent applied glass vines and leaves; 2½" high; early signature; inscribed: "T. G. C." (Tiffany Glass Co.)

In 1870, at the age of twenty-two, he was elected to membership in the Century Club; in 1871, he became an Associate Member of the National Academy of Design; and in 1880, he was made a full Academician.

While exhibiting his paintings at the Philadelphia Centennial Exposition in 1876, he became intensely aware of the work of decorative artists, and inspired by stained glass windows he had seen in Europe, he began to experiment with the actual making of stained glass.

Eventually he developed a glass that could be manipulated to imitate the form and draping of fabrics without further external painting or "shading" on the glass. In 1878, he set up his own glasshouse and engaged a Venetian glassblower, Andrea Boldini, to supervise the furnaces. Though both this and a subsequently-built factory burned down, he continued experiments and production at the Heidt glasshouse in Brooklyn, New York, from 1880 to 1893.

The Philadelphia Centennial had

Nasturtium vase, a magnificant example of this difficult technique; flowers are pale orange, floating amongst leaves of deep bottle green and dark blue; inner surface of vase is iridized. Marked "L. C. Tiffany-Favrile, No. No. 3595N."

Left to Right: Mandarin yellow opalescent vase, red *art nouveau* swirl decoration; inner surface iridized in gold; H. 5½''; inscribed: L. C. Tiffany-Favrile No. 7797A. Claret red vase with apple green paperweight flowers and leaves; iridescent inner surface; H. 10¾''; inscribed: L. C. Tiffany-Favrile No. 8824L. Black iridescent bowl vase with amber iridescent leaves and vines; H. 3¼''; inscribed: L. C. T. No. Q585.

also renewed public interest in Candace Wheeler's Society of Decorative Art, a group which encouraged women possessing artistic talent to market their work. Mr. Tiffany collaborated with this society until 1879. Then, manifesting his desire to lead rather than follow, he formed his own company with Samuel Coleman, Lockwood DeForrest, and Mrs. Wheeler, who was persuaded to join him. This he called "Louis C. Tiffany Co., Associated Artists."

Sophisticated New Yorkers were enchanted with Tiffany's new style of decorating, and for the next four years he devoted himself feverishly to the complete interior decoration of fashionable homes and public institutions. He used his beloved stained glass wherever possible, and introduced glass mosaics and tiles in fireplaces and decorative screens. Rugs, tapestries, upholstery fabrics, embroideries, wallpapers, and furniture were all designed and produced by his firm of talented artists.

Mrs. Wheeler left the organization in 1883, taking with her the department of needlework and her original name, "Associated Artists." Mr. Tiffany then formed the "Tiffany Glass Co.," concentrating on stained glass windows for interiors and churches.

In 1892, he again reorganized and expanded. The firm became the "Tiffany Glass and Decorating Co.," and construction was started on a glass factory in Corona, Long Island.

Beginnings of Favrile

It has been said Louis Tiffany developed his Favrile glass ornamental wares because of the tremendous amount of waste glass which accumulated during the making of his windows. This is plausible, but mere practicality seems strangely out-of-scale with the pattern of Tiffany's life. It would, in my opinion, seem entirely logical that he preferred to adorn his houses and interiors with objects and art born of his own talent rather than draw upon the style of others. The name he coined derived from the root word *faber,* meaning "handmade," softened first to *Fabrile,* then to *Favrile.*

The new Tiffany furnaces were in operation by the end of 1893, and Arthur J. Nash, a glass manufacturer from Stourbridge, England, was engaged to supervise the glass-blowing division. Mr. Tiffany *personally over-*

seered all beginning production, and after introducing the various craftsmen to his style and color preferences, would then allow them to develop the object to their interpretation of his original concept. He was a relentless taskmaster, however, and so asserted his personality that each piece, though often interpreted by many craftsmen, bears his distinct mark.

Since profit was not his prime concern, he encouraged experimenting, advising his glassblowers to work and rework a piece in the hope that an accidental effect would produce that little bit of magic he so earnestly

Miniature gold "tear bottle" in most unusual Cypriote technique, a replica of buried, ancient glass; 3¾" high; inscribed: "L. C. Tiffany-Favrile."

Yellow agate glass vase with cut panels and carved fish; H. 3¾"; inscribed: 103A-Coll. L. C. Tiffany-Favrile. Extremely rare carved glass vase; brilliant lemon yellow background with pale green Iris leaf pattern; H. 5½"; inscribed: L. C. Tiffany-Favrile No. 5504M. Exhibition Piece.

desired. His earliest pieces, therefore, are of a tremendous variety of shapes, and bear little resemblance to what the non-collector recognizes as Tiffany glass.

Shapes, in the beginning, were generally based on Islamic and Oriental forms or on the "nature and growth" principle of the *art nouveau* movement then in full vogue. Thus it would seem that no pieces of early Tiffany could be alike.

Contrary to what has been said, few, if any, of these earlier pieces were signed. Some were simply inscribed with an "x" or "o", followed by a number. This is a type most sought by advanced collectors today.

Intrigued by the iridescent quality of ancient, excavated glass, he experimented with chemicals to reproduce its effect. The final result was achieved by a chemical spray which emitted fumes on the hot glass when it was taken from the furnace. The resulting iridescence fused with the glass and became an integral part of it. The exact formula for this technique was kept secret.

Collectors are most familiar with the iridized glass, and it is this type which has become almost synonymous with the name Tiffany. Though hues of gold or blue were most profusely produced, almost every color was made and iridized during some phase of production.

Tiffany Signatures

Not until about 1900 was the glass consistently signed, and pieces produced which could be matched and remade in quantity. Tableware, for

Left to Right: Extremely rare red opalescent vase with gunmetal striping, white casing; H. 12¼''; inscribed: L. C. Tiffany-Favrile No. 5593E. Red gourd-shaped vase, raisin brown design, white inner casing; H. 6¾''; inscribed: L. C. Tiffany-Favrile No. 551K. Red paperweight vase with brown leaves and vines; entire inner surface iridized in red; H. 7¾''; inscribed: L. C. Tiffany-Favrile No. 9452H.

example, was then given pattern names, as advertised in Tiffany & Co.'s *Blue Books*. We can be certain that by 1904 every piece was supposed to have been signed, for the *Blue Book* for that year reads: "As this unique glass is being imitated and inferior products are represented as 'Favrile Glass' or 'Tiffany Glass,' patrons are cautioned to look for the distinguishing mark on every piece of Tiffany Favrile Glass, *Louis C. Tiffany* or *L.C.T.*"

The signature is often preceded or followed by a number, with a letter in front or after it. The exact meaning of letters and numbers is not yet known; collectors and museum curators are still conducting research. A signature does not in any way indicate the quality or rarity of the glass; a simple piece of gold tableware may have the full signature while a very rare paperweight vase could be signed merely "L.C.T."

Tiffany Techniques

Exact formulas for Tiffany glass are lost to us, since all processes were held in absolute secrecy. Techniques are numberless; variety and originality were rules rather than exceptions. No single formula could em-

Lava vase in deep brown and earth greens; design melts away in some places to "window" the middle layer and sometimes shows the iridescent inner surface; H. 6½"; inscribed: 51A-Coll. L. G. Tiffany-Favrile.

brace such wide variations as the mundane gold iridescent salt dish and the supreme "flower-form," whose technique drew upon no other culture or era of glassmaking.

Carved or cameo glass was also produced, the subject matter of design being mostly floral. Paperweight glass was made with flowers, leaves, or vines "growing" between layers of glass, occasionally with the inner surface of the vase iridized. "Aquamarine" paperweight vases were blown of heavy clear glass with undersea motifs, fish, and lily pads, trapped in the solid mass of glass. These are generally completely uniridized, as are many vases in the more dynamic hues of red, yellow, brown, etc.

There is never any external decoration of Tiffany glass other than the glass itself; the flowers, carving, swirling, or iridescence are all homogeneous. Though some Tiffany glass has been found with external decoration or silver mountings, it is safe to assume that this was done by other firms after the object had been sold.

The exception is seen in the silver-mounted perfume bottles and small wares with silver caps which were sold through Tiffany & Co. The silver, however, is *always* marked "Tiffany & Co." (Tiffany & Co., the silver and jewelry store, was never associated with Louis Tiffany's enterprises except as an additional outlet for the sale of his glass.)

In 1900, Tiffany Glass and Decorating Co. reorganized as "Tiffany Studios," to lead the field in the production of electric lamps with leaded and stained glass shades. Though best known for Favrile, The Studios also designed and produced pottery, enamels, bronzes, and jewelry.

As the vogue for Tiffany glass spread, rival companies began to imitate it, especially the gold and blue iridescent types; none achieved the artistry of the originator. When less desirable imitations began to flood the market, Mr. Tiffany withdrew his support from the Studios. Mr. Nash continued to operate the furnaces, but he lacked the necessary funds, and the quality of the glass steadily declined.

Louis Comfort Tiffany died January 17, 1933, having devoted his long lifetime to the arts.

English Iridescent Glass

by C. C. MANLEY

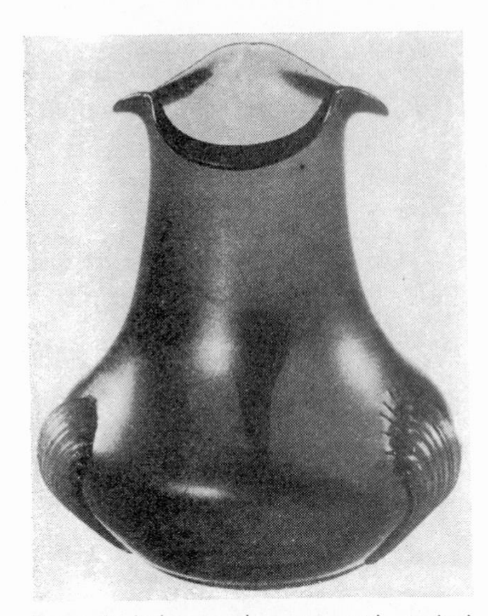

Figure 1: Iridescent glass vase with applied shell decoration. Thomas Webb & Sons, ca. 1900. Height 6"; weight 1 lb. 2 oz.

IT IS GENERALLY ACCEPTED that iridescent glass, as we know it today, originated in Bohemia about 1878. This is probably true, but in the Crystal Palace Exhibition of 1851, Lloyd & Summerfield of Birmingham, England, exhibited glass vases and other objects of such coloring that the descriptions of them given in the exhibition catalog seem to imply an iridescent surface. In any case, Mr. Summerfield of Lloyd & Summerfield, traveled extensively on the Continent and had many opportunities to discuss glass with European glassmakers.

Although Stourbridge was responsible for some very attractive specimens, some of the most extraordinary and beautiful examples of iridescent glass originated on the Continent. But it is English iridescent glass we wish to identify, most of which was produced in the Midlands — the cheaper kind in Birmingham, art varieties in the Stourbridge district. Since this type of glass was made in enormous quantities, and in half a dozen countries, the task of identifying Stourbridge specimens is, to say the least, problematical. If it were not for the English glassmaking techniques and design characteristics, the task would be impossible.

We would suggest that collectors read Albert Christian Revi's book, *Nineteenth Century Glass—Its Genesis and Development* (Thomas Nelson & Sons, 1959 and 1967). This book contains a very informative chapter on iridescent glass, and could act as a basis for future study.

In the early 1880s, iridescent glass was being made by a number of firms in Stourbridge, Thomas Webb & Sons being possibly the first. After a few years of experimenting, Webb came up with the renowned "Bronze Glass." This type of iridescent glass is of outstanding beauty and quality and exceedingly scarce.

Figure 2: Bronze glass vase with handles (purple sheen). Thomas Webb & Sons, ca. 1880. Height 7½"; weight 1 lb. 5 oz.

Figure 3: Bronze glass vase with handles (purple sheen). Thomas Webb & Sons, ca. 1880. Height 8 1/2"; weight 3 lbs. 11 oz.

As Webb made both Iridescent and Bronze glass during the same period, the collector's first task is to learn to separate the two types, for Bronze glass is worth as many dollars as Iridescent glass is worth nickels.

Little difficulty should be experienced in telling these wares apart. Iridescent glass is always lighter in weight and the surface is rarely mold decorated. Applied decorations are sometimes found on iridescent wares, the most common being a shell motif having 15 points *(Figure 1)*. We believe the shell decoration to be exclusively Webb's, and it was applied in a number of colors. Another applied decoration found on Iridescent glass consists of applied "drops." These again are in many colors, some having a second color over the first.

The way the pontil mark is ground is another aid to identification. Since the base of the iridescent object is rather thin, the original pontil scar is usually not ground out. The top of the object may be straight or wavy, but never ground flat. Enamel decorations — and this includes gilt — are not plentiful; those which were used are mostly of a floral type and generally depict common garden flowers.

All these means of identification apply only when the color of the iridescence is the same as Webb's Bronze glass. Webb's record book of 1878 refers to green as well as bronze, both colors being produced in plain and crackled effects. The type of crackling is unique — we have never seen its duplicate in any other glass. The crackling marks are hair-like in appearance, very close together and at times they come to the surface of the glass, making it feel rough.

Three types of Bronze glass were made at the Webb factory. One with a plain surface followed shapes of antique Roman and Greek vessels; these were very heavy, the thickness of the sides in some cases being approximately one-half inch *(Figures 2 and 3)*. Another type, with a molded surface, was a little more decorative, and would be no more than twice the weight of a piece of Webb's Iridescent glass of comparable size and shape. The shell decoration was often applied to this type of Bronze glass. The third type, rather humorous in character, with an owl's head formed on the surface, nearly always had enamel decorations *(Figure 4)*. Officially, bronze and green were the only colors used at the Webb factory for their Bronze glass, but old employees have told us that all colors were tried, though in what quantity they could not say. We have never seen any bearing Webb's mark.

The pontil mark is not ground out in the heavy type of Bronze glass, but is ground out in both the others. In common with Webb's Iridescent glass, the tops of all three varieties of Bronze glass were never ground flat.

Possibly inspired by the success of Webb's Bronze glass, John Northwood, working for Richardsons, produced a ware similar to Webb's Bronze glass. If not better looking, it is certainly more scarce. It has a molded surface and is quite as heavy as Webb's heaviest glass. The glass itself is of a green similar to Webb's but the lustrous surface reflection is a deep purple color.

We were told by a relative of John Northwood that when this type of

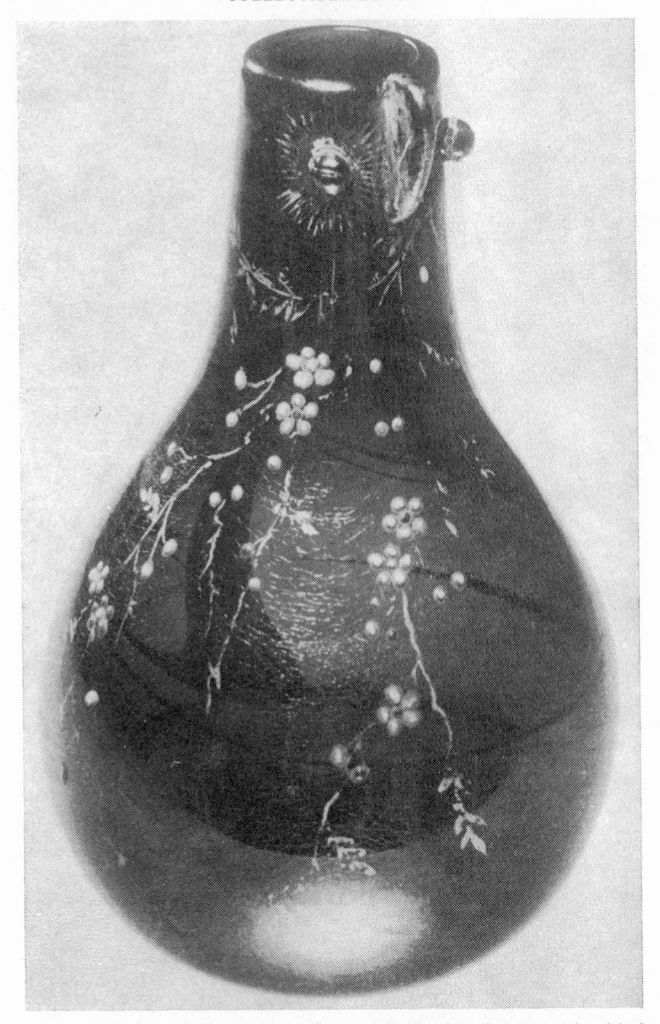

Figure 4: Webb Bronze glass vase with applied owl face and gilded decoration. The slightly crackled effect in the glass is reflected in the lustrous surface sheen. Ca. 1890. Height 7¼"; weight 1 lb.

iridescent glass was being made, the fumes generated by the lustering compound were so bad that the men working in the factory refused to continue. Be that as it may, all specimens of Northwood's iridescent glass seem to have been acquired by the Northwood family.

In November 1963, Sotheby's sold at auction in their London galleries two pieces of iridescent glass described in their catalog as of "a dark green iridescent glass simulating the texture of a brain." This was a perfect description of the outer surface of the vases, thus "Brain Glass" *(Figure 5).* The few pieces we have examined are so crude that it seems to emphasize the great difficulties encountered in their making. Once a piece of Webb's Bronze glass with the molded surface *(Figure 6)* is compared to Richardsons' "Brain Glass," no difficulty will be found in identifying either. A large vase in Richardsons' Brain Glass is exhibited in the Brierley Hill Council House collection.

Richardsons experimented with iridescent glass more than any other Stourbridge firm. The result was a

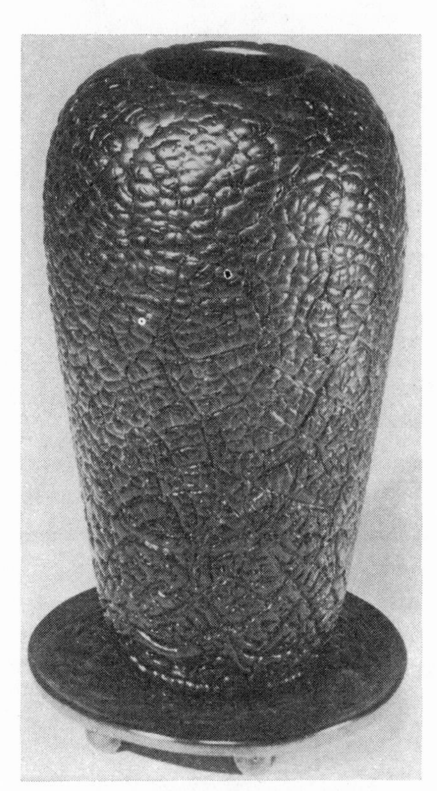

Figure 5: Vase and stand in Richardsons' "Brain Glass" (deep purple sheen); ca. 1890. Height 14½"; weight 10 lbs. 8 oz.

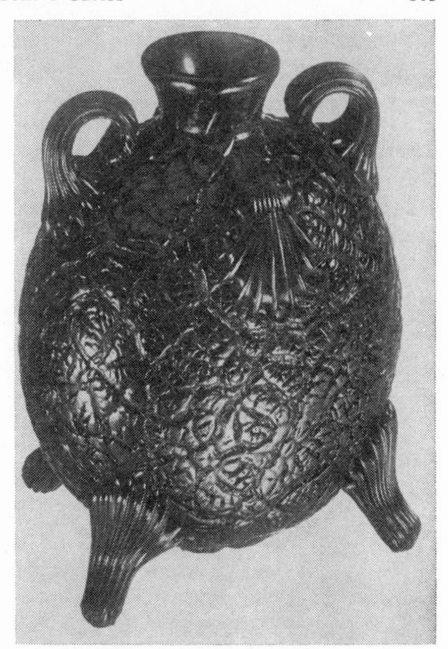

Figure 6: Footed vase with handles in Webb's Bronze glass (purple sheen); ca. 1880. Compare the textured surface of this object with Richardsons' "Brain Glass" vase shown in Figure 5. Height 7"; weight 2 lbs. 2 oz.

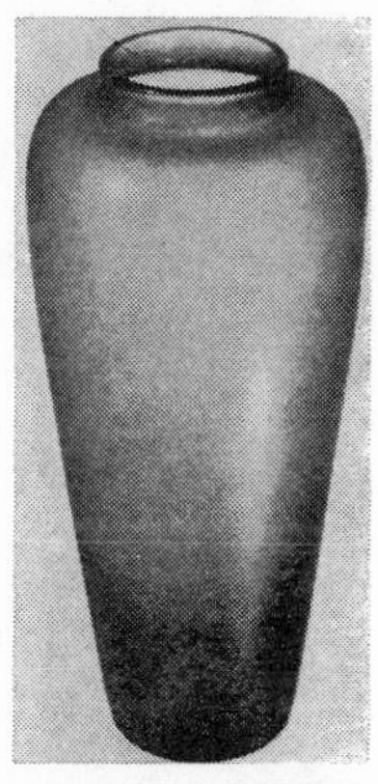

Fig. 7: Richardsons' Iridescent Crystal vase with matt finish. Ca. 1910. Height 10"; weight 1 lb. 2 oz.

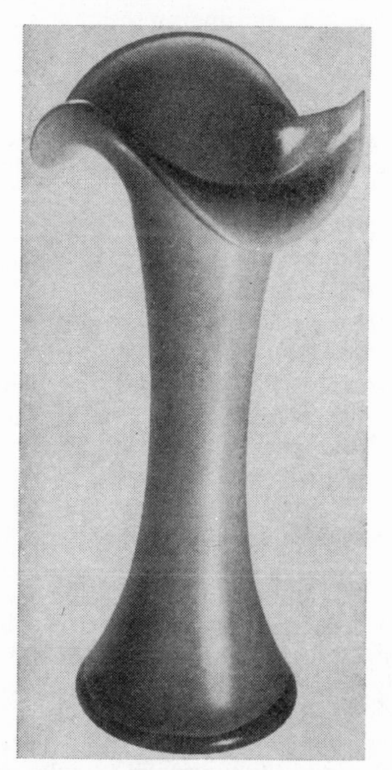

Figure 8: Richardsons' Pearl Iridescent vase—Opaline or Alabaster glass cased with crystal and iridized; ca. 1910. Height 6½"; weight 8 oz.

number of rare and special pieces. One type, outstanding for its simplicity of shape and its iridized surface, is shown in *Figure 7*. The base is of lead crystal and fairly heavy. The surface is perfectly smooth; the color, being more slate than purple, has a matt finish, and all reflections are neutralized. This "Neutral Tint" is a rather pleasing effect. The manufacturing difficulties incurred in the production of this type of lustred glass must have been many, for we can find no evidence of other Stourbridge firms producing an article with a similar surface finish.

Richardsons also produced a number of commercial lines of pearl iridescence *(Figures 8 and 9)*. The procedure for making their most expensive type of iridescent ware was to coat their Opaline or Alabaster glass with a crystal overlay and then to iridize the surface. The finished article looked exactly like mother-of-pearl. Some bowls and vases were decorated with applied glass snakes and lizards before the iridizing process was finished. Specimens of this type of Pearl Iridescent glass are very rare.

It's essential that the collector become familiar with one of Richardsons' commercial lines of Pearl Iridescent glass, for it is very much like a ware made in Czechoslovakia. Both were blown in a dip mold, the surface pattern, resembling a six-sided honeycomb, is raised, and the coloring is identical *(Figure 9)*.

Now for the difference: The English type is very much heavier and a great many pieces have applied rings and drops in various colors. Also, the top is scalloped which, together with other hand manipulation of the object, tends to distort the pattern in the glass towards the top. The Czech version of this ware does not have these characteristics and is much lighter in weight.

Crystal glass objects were also iridized, but these wares do not usually command a high price. The colors are somewhat insipid, too.

Stevens & Williams of Brierley Hill made a great deal of iridescent glass,

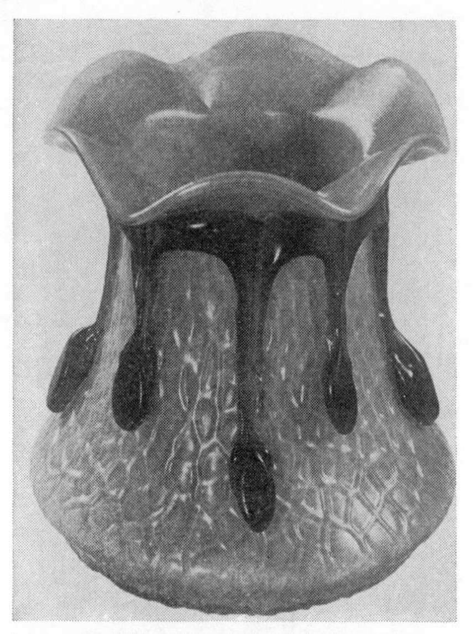

Figure 9: Richardsons' Pearl Iridescent vase with molded honeycomb decoration is identical to some pieces of Czechoslovakian glass of the same period; ca. 1925. Height 5"; weight 1 lb. 4 oz.

but we have found few pieces of real merit. The possible exception to this appraisal might be their Iridescent Alabaster glass. Unlike Richardsons' Pearl Iridescent glass, this did not have a crystal overlay or casing.

For the collector who wishes to identify Stevens & Williams iridescent crystal wares, the color, which is brown, will be found around the top of the object, be it bowl, sugar basin, or salt cellar. Stevens & Williams pattern-molded opalescent vaseline-colored glass was sometimes iridized, but the iridescence appears unnecessary on such a beautiful glass.

Because iridescent glass was so easy to make, the small one-man businesses (called "Cribs" in England) produced a fair amount of this ware, too. The products from these sources are of little value to the collector, but they certainly add to the difficulties when an attempt is made at identification.

Originally, manufacturers tried to mix the metallic lustering oxides with their glass melts, but they soon discovered that the various oxides could be applied to the surface of the articles using a cheaper and easier method. After the object was formed it was placed in a chamber into which the fumes of various oxides were blown. The fumes attacked and/or attached themselves to the surface of the glass, resulting in a highly iridescent finish. Up to a point, the length of time the objects were left in the chamber determined the degree of iridescence.

Another common method used to produce somewhat the same results was to paint a lustering compound on the surface of the glass while it was being worked at the furnace mouth and was still in a plastic state. The easiest, cheapest, and most common

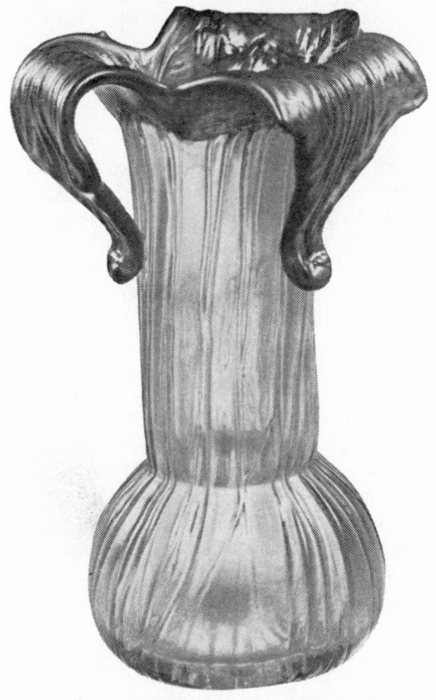

Figure 10: An onion-shaped iridescent glass vase, probably made by Lloyd & Summerfield of Birmingham, England; ca. 1870. Height 6½"; weight 1 lb. 1 oz.

method of iridizing glass was to spray a metallic solution on the glass before it went through the annealing ovens (lehr). Obviously, the depth of the iridized surface is very shallow and, as Frederick Carder of Steuben commented after examining some iridescent glass made in Czechoslovakia, "Rub it hard enough and the color will come off."

The author's investigation into the iridescent glasses made in Birmingham and the surrounding area failed to uncover much of collectible quality. Birmingham manufacturers, whatever their products, have always been "production minded." Glass manufacturers in this area were no exception. Most of them accepted the Czechoslovakian challenge of iridescent glass, and their mimicry of these foreign wares makes it virtually impossible to differentiate between the two products. One Birmingham firm, Lloyd & Summerfield, Park Glassworks, Spring Hill, seems to be the manufacturer of a series of vases in the shapes and colors of onions and leeks *(Figure 10)*, the surface being iridized.

One last word to the keen collector. Practically every type of British iridescent glassware has been iridized on the outside, but some has been treated on the inside only. Occasionally a piece is found where a surface pattern has been attempted by controlling the fumes from the metallic oxides. Objects with pull-up threaded decorations were favorite specimens for iridescent wares. As Continental glass of this same type was made in exactly the same way as English glassware (threaded from the bottom upward), only the country's traditional shapes can be a guide to identification and attribution.

Intarsia, Graal and Ariel Glass

by *ALBERT CHRISTIAN REVI*

Graal glass vase of Edward Hald. Collection Orrefors Glass Works.

Intarsia vase by Frederick Carder. Collection of the author.

FROM 1916 to 1923 Frederick Carder, co-founder of the Steuben Glass Works at Corning, N. Y., produced artistic-glassware emulating those decorative designs created by inlaying wood in a background of wood and known as "intarsia." To make his intarsia glasses, Carder formed a small bulb of glass on the end of an iron and coated it with any desired color. The colored casing was then etched into a pattern. Thereafter, the bulb was reheated slowly, picked up on the blow iron, and blown out larger. It was then blown into a cup of crystal glass made to receive it, and the two, cohering, were blown out to the shape and size required. The stem or foot was attached and the article annealed.

In 1917 the Orrefors Glassworks of Orrefors, Sweden, featured a display of Simon Gates' Graal glass at Nordiska Kompaniet, a department store in Stockholm. The Graal glass consisted of several thin layers of colored glass, cleverly etched into pleasing designs and plated with a skin of crystal glass to leave a smooth exterior. In the 1930's Vicke Lindstrand and Edward Hald of Orrefors revamped the Graal technique, applying a thick layer of colored glass, the decorative pattern being reflected in a striking play of colors.

At an exhibition in Paris in 1937, Edvin Ohrstrom's Ariel glass made its appearance. The new Ariel glass resembled the Graal technique, but differed in its use of patterns of bubbles as part of the decoration. Interesting figure and flower compositions, rich in color, were combined with the silvery gleam of air bubbles to give a scintilating texture.

During the nineteenth century several patents were issued covering similar decorative productions in glass. On May 25, 1850, Edward Pettitt of Birmingham, England, registered his method for rolling plates of window glass with ornamental designs sandwiched between two layers of glass. Pieces of colored glass which had been previously stamped, cast, or cut into ornamental forms were applied to a sheet of glass and thereafter another sheet of glass was either cast or rolled over the ornamental design. Pettitt suggested in his enumerations that (1) the colored pattern could be applied to a background of opaque white or colored glass, or (2) a pattern could be drawn on a plate of glass with plumbago and connected to a galvanic battery for the purpose of depositing a metallic design which would afterward be covered with another layer of glass.

On April 6, 1853, "a communication from abroad" was registered at the Patent Offices in London by William Johnson of Glasgow, Scotland. (Mr. Johnson acted as agent only, and a careful search of the patent records offers no clue to the actual patentee). The invention related to the production of ornamental surfaces by incrustation or "inlaid work (intarsia)." Two pieces of different colored glass, laid one upon the other, were united by heat; they were then softened in an enamelling furnace, and a design of any kind impressed on their surfaces. By this means the upper colored piece was squeezed into, and partially penetrated, the lower one according to the design on the impressing die. The entire surface was then ground flat and the superfluous glass cut away, leaving the actual design imbedded in the lower piece of glass.

In another method, the die employed was simply a punch corresponding in outline to the contour of the design. A number of plates of glass of uniform thickness, but of different colors, were perforated by this punch, and the pieces so cut out were exchanged and inserted into corresponding holes in the different plates. Thus, a piece cut from a blue plate was inserted into an opening in a red plate, while the piece from the red plate was inserted into the corresponding opening of the blue plate, and so on throughout the series, with different colored glasses being inlaid together to form varied and colorful designs. The intarsia techniques registered by William Johnson represent a rare and interesting development in pressed glass.

Achille Lemaire of Paris, France, registered his means for producing intarsia glass July 14, 1879. The patent received only provisional protection at the London Patent Offices. Etching an applied colored layer of glass prior to applying a second skin of glass, as Carder has done, was one of his suggestions.

On November 8, 1883, Lewis John Murray of the Soho and Vesta Glass Works, Birmingham, England, registered a means for producing intarsia glass closely resembling the procedure used by Frederick Carder and Simon Gates. Murray etched, engraved, or sand-blasted the design on a blow, plated with colored glass, before blowing it into a cup of glass, thereby entrapping the colored design between two layers of clear crystal glass. He registered his patent in America on December 23, 1884.

There are relatively few factories in operation today that can boast such intricate productions as intarsia, Graal, and Ariel glass. Consequently, the entire industry views with pride the artistic contributions of such twentieth century craftsmen as Carder, Gates, Lindstrand, Hald, and Ohrstrom.

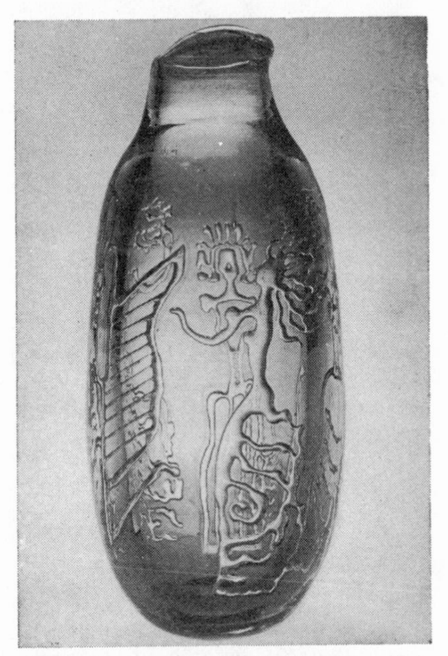

Ariel glass vase by Edvin Ohrstrom. Collection Orrefors Glass Works.

Gray-Stan Glass, 1926-1936

by ALBERT CHRISTIAN REVI

Ashtray in clear amber glass, 2¾" high; pinched vase in clear glass, smudges of Bristol blue in the body, 5" high. Billinghurst Collection.

EARLY in 1926, a very remarkable Irishwoman, Mrs. Graydon-Stannus, F.R.S.A., established a small glasshouse in the heart of London. Mrs. Stannus was a very knowledgeable person in the field of glass, with ideas of her own on the subject. She established the factory to put these ideas into practice; within a very few years Gray-Stan art glass had gained an international reputation. As early as 1928, her glass was distributed in America through Messrs. Kay & Ellinger, 30 Irving Place, New York City. In Kelly's Directories from 1928 to 1933, the firm of "Graystan Glass" was listed with their location —69 & 71 High Street, Battersea, London S.W. 11; from 1934 to 1936, it was described as "Gray-Stan Glass" (note difference in spelling), with Exhibition Showrooms at 14a Pont Street, London, S.W. 1.

About a year prior to the opening of her little glass factory, Mrs. Stannus gathered around her a small party of glass technicians, and told them of her desire and plans to produce a superior kind of art glass, different from that being produced by English contemporaries. Suitable premises were found, consisting of a double-fronted shop with living quarters above and a spacious covered yard at the back, with a gate into the side street. One of the shops was used for a stockroom, the other as office and studio. The living quarters housed the caretaker.

The brick wall around the yard and the roof were repaired, and a furnace capable of holding four crucibles (three large and one small) was built, also an annealing oven, shelves, and benches. In one corner of the yard, above the ground level, was built a mixing shed where raw ingredients for the glass batches were prepared. Under this, at ground level, was the storage space for the fuel (coke).

When everything was completed, a series of trials was carried out successfully and the little Gray-Stan factory started production on High Street early in 1926. There was a day and a night shift. James Manning was chief blower by day, with three servitors. George Hollins headed the night shift as chief blower, with two servitors. The servitors were competent blowers in their own right and quite often the chief blower would take a break by handing his chair to an assistant while he himself acted as servitor. Initiative was never stifled. On the contrary a chair was always at the disposal of anyone who wished to try out an inspiration. Mrs. Stannus encouraged the men in this and, as an example of latent artistry so discovered, would point with pride to the remarkable results achieved by "a bright-eyed rascal from the slums of Lambeth" who, after three short months as an apprentice, was put in the chair one dinner hour and told to "get on with it."

Gray-Stan started with 12 to 14 workers of all grades. This number was increased with the business to 37, then decreased as work slackened. About 30 men were working in the factory when it closed in 1936.

All Gray-Stan glass was made to a lead formula and in the following colors: colorless transparent glass (crystal), transparent amber, blue, green, and red glass, plain or molded; or a combination of two or more colors as a definite pattern, or graduated. Opalescent glass in the above colors, and a solid blue (Bristol) decorated with aventurine crumbs were also produced. Great success was achieved with their combination of glass and china enamel.

Their experiments with the glass and china enamel combinations were troublesome, but eventually, after adjusting temperatures and changing the glass formula, they achieved their aim. Some of the early pieces of this particular ware were interesting because the color had gone wrong during the annealing. Nevertheless, these were sold, but with the strict understanding they could not be repeated. Gray-Stan's china enamel glassware resembles the Clutha and Cluthra glasses made by James Couper & Sons of Glasgow, ca. 1899, and Fred Carder of the Steuben Glass Works, ca. 1925. (See SW, Dec. '62). Collectors will have little trouble differentiating between the three wares, as almost always, each bears the mark of its manufacturer.

Mrs. Stannus had some difficulty in registering her trademark of a harp and the words "Gray-Stan Glass," but it was eventually attained and her wares bear the signature "Gray-Stan" or "Graystan."

Some of the glass beakers, plaques, urns, and bowls which were made at Gray-Stan, in all sizes and colors, show a combination of all colors in one article. The head designer, A. Noel Billinghurst, created designs for their carved glass, another specialty of this enterprising industry. This owed nothing to machinery in its fashioning. The figures were mostly classical in inspiration, and the designs penetrated right through the glass. Stones and gems were copied in glass, the most successful being lapis lazuli, Mexican and Chinese jade, and Mexican agate. The London *Evening News* for March 5, 1931, reported that men preferred Gray-Stan's topaz and agate glass, while women fancied the cloud effects of their china enamel glass, allied colors, or jade.

Mrs. Stannus surrounded herself with talented craftsmen. Manning, Hollins, and an experienced glass cutter named Everet were not youngsters, but men with years of experience in traditional blowing and cutting, from which they did not find it easy to break away. Nevertheless, they were very willing to try Mrs. Stannus' ideas and, in doing so, attained great artistic heights.

The situation with James Manning and George Hollins was both interesting and convenient. Manning was an artist and creator in glass. After a discussion of a new idea he would have the ways and means worked

Gray-Stan bowl, 13" dia., in deep purple glass with white threads. **Victoria & Albert Museum.**

out pat in his mind, and without further ado would be back at his chair working like fury. If asked to repeat the design, he could do it but, for him, it would be quite laborious. Hollins, on the other hand, could not readily form a mental picture from a talk, but if given a drawing or prototype, he could turn out any number with almost mechanical precision. The combination of the two men was a happy one for Gray-Stan.

After the factory had been producing some time, it was realized that some of the pontil marks on the bases of various items were sharp and could inflict a nasty cut when being handled. A small cutting shed was rigged up, and with Mr. Everet and an assistant as cutters, all pontil marks were ground and smoothed out from then on. After initiating a junior in this task, Mr. Everet was free to cut brilliant patterns in the traditional sense, though the factory was trying to break away from the customary. Mr. Billinghurst always did his own glass carving to his original designs.

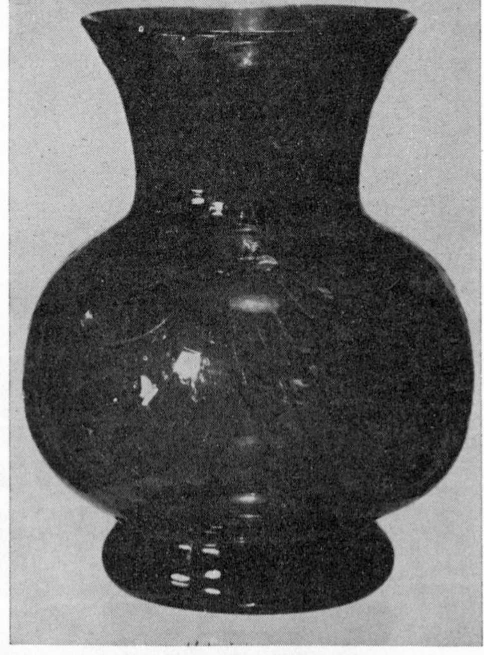

Fan-shaped vase, glass and china enamel, in mottled turquoise blue, 8". Vase of deep Bristol blue glass with threads of glass and aventurine speckles, 10¼". Carved crystal glass vase, 7", engraved by A. Noel Billinghurst. Billinghurst Collection.

Frequent meetings of the whole staff were called to discuss new ideas, ways, and means. No suggestions were ever rejected out of hand, even though offered by a junior. There was no boss or foreman in the literal sense. When Mrs. Stannus was away, Mr. Billinghurst held the reins. It was a shop where each employee worked happily at his own special job, ever ready to help in any other capacity, no matter how menial.

In an address to the Royal Society of Arts (London, February 13, 1925), Mrs. Stannus described her wares as "New Irish Glass," asserting that though the glass was, in fact, made in London, it was manufactured from old Irish recipes, by Irishmen, and she, herself, was Irish. She also admitted to this distinguished group of glass manufacturers and artists that when things went wrong in the factory—a not uncommon occurrence in glasshouses, "I abuse the men in a flood of Irish denunciation in a rich brogue."

She said her endeavor was to create, not copy, and this criterion had formulated the company's motto, "Gray-Stan Does Not Copy—It Creates." All Gray-Stan glass was made entirely by hand. Because she believed "nothing kills individuality in an artist so much as machinery," no mechanical aids of any kind were used in the factory. Fortunately they did possess some very fine old molds which had become smoothed or softened by years of use. When the first pieces were produced, she showed them to her clientele for old Irish glass, and found they had ideas of their own of the sort of wares they would like to buy. She set to work to meet their requirements, and a week after they had asked for a dessert service, or a set of candlesticks, she delivered their requests. Hers was an advantage over big manufacturers whose organizations could be upset by special orders.

She attributed the "difference" of her glassware from that of her contemporaries to the fact her glass was hand-fashioned; no two pieces in a set being exactly alike. Successfully, she shaded colors to gain pastel effects, added threads and bits of colored splosh which melted into the surface of the article while it was being worked at the furnace. Some pieces were passed through two or three molds, getting an impression of each mold on it with pleasing results.

So impressive were the wares made at Gray-Stan that Mrs. Stannus had the honor of making and presenting to the Queen's Doll House, their chandeliers, wall lights, table candlesticks and a miniature table service consisting of plates, goblets, finger bowls, etc. Special wheels were made to effect the cutting and polishing of the tiny chandeliers.

Gray-Stan's business was good up to 1929/30. Then trade began to slacken, due in part to the reaction of financial distress in the United States. (Gray-Stan had been doing a very good American business.) It hobbled along for a little while, but near the end of 1936, this unique venture in glass manufacturing came to an end.

Schneider Art Glass

by JOHN W. GRAVES

THE Cristallerie Schneider was established in 1903 by two brothers, Charles and Ernest Schneider, at Epinay-sur-Seine, in the Department of Seine, about seven miles from Paris, France. The glassworks operated at this location until 1962 when it was moved to the small town of Lorris, in the Department of Loiert, near Orleans, France. The factory moved to avail itself of the natural gas fuel which is distributed at Lorris but not in the area of Paris. The Schneider works is still in operation today.

Art glass was made by the Schneider firm from 1903 to 1930. Between 1930 and 1945, the firm made glass of very light and transparent colors, such as smoked and amber shades, in addition to clear crystal wares. Since 1945 only clear crystal has been produced.

Charles Schneider was the art director and supervisor of the art glass department during the entire period it was active. He made many of the beautiful pieces himself. Most of their art glass wares were made by men

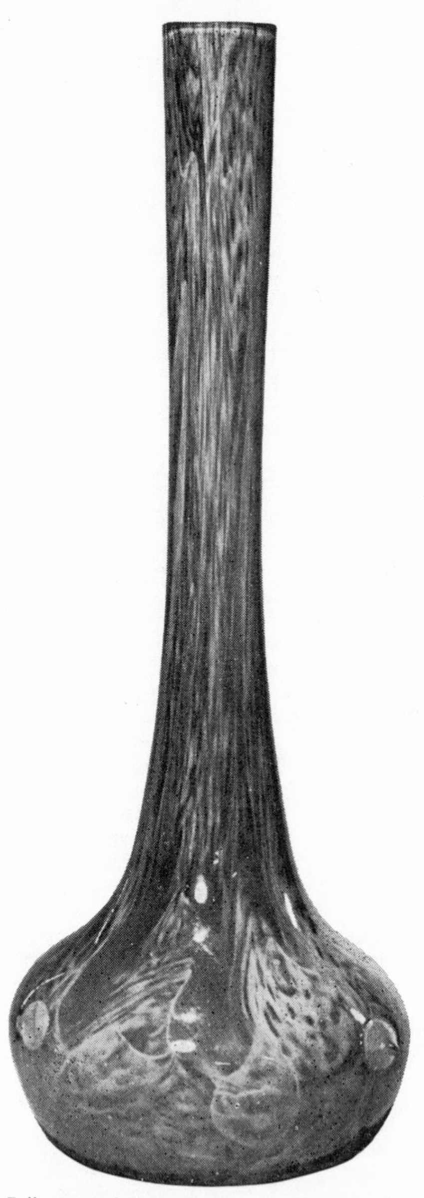

Tall vase of three layers of glass—swirled cranberry-red, crystal, and swirled yellow; three applied yellow prunts around base. Height 22 inches.

Vase of cloudy yellow glass with mauve-colored pull-up design in base, cranberry-red lining; applied pinched decorations in orange-colored glass at sides; height 6 inches.

who were taught by Charles Schneider, and they followed his designs and instructions to the letter.

Charles Schneider was born in Nancy, in the Department of Muerthe and Moselle, in 1881. He studied under Emile Gallé at the school of fine arts in Nancy. During this period he also worked at the Gallé factory, and for a time he was a designer for the Daum brothers of Nancy, France. Later, Schneider studied at *l'Ecole des Beaux Arts* in Paris. He was a member of the jury, and therefore a non-competitor, at the International Exposition of Decorative Arts in 1925, where Lalique, Marinot, and Orrefors had important glass exhibits. Because of his many accomplishments in the fields of art and glassmaking he was honored as a *Chevalier de la Legion D'Honneur*—a French order of merit instituted by Napoleon Bonaparte in 1802. This honor is conferred upon both men and women, Frenchman or foreigner, for outstanding achievements in military or civilian life. Charles Schneider lived in the family's long-time residence at 87 Av. Jean-Jaures, in Epinay-sur-Seine. He died in 1962.

Ernest Schneider, who was two years older than his brother, was the business manager and administrator of the firm. Their father, who was a railroad official, died when Charles and Ernest were only four and six years old.

In 1944, the art direction for the firm was taken over by Charles Schneider's son, Robert Schneider, who was born in 1917. He, too, had studied at *l'Ecole des Beaux Arts* in Paris, and was a winner of the *Prix de Rome*—an award given annually by the French government to students of the fine arts. Robert Schneider is still in charge of all design and production at the Schneider glassworks. Except for Robert Schneider, only one of the men trained by Charles Schneider remains in an active position at the factory; this man

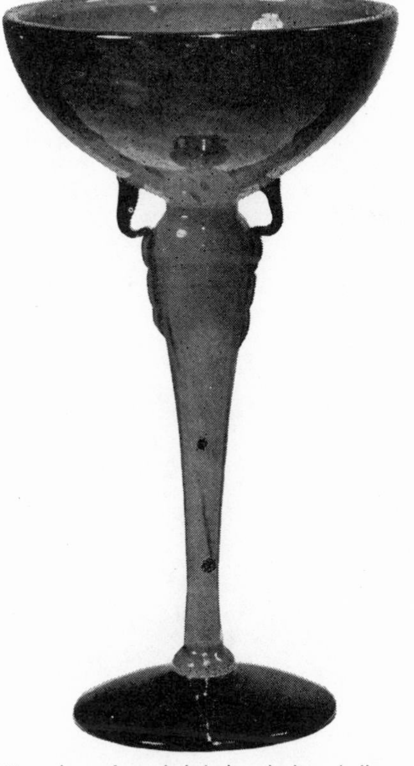

Wine glass of mottled dark red glass, hollow red stem; foot and applied decorations of amethyst-colored glass; height 8 inches.

Console set of mottled blue and orange glass; foot of compote is amethyst glass with "candy stripes." Candlesticks, 13 inches tall.

Vase of iridescent red (Rouge Flambe) glass; height 10 inches.

An example of Schneider's cameo glass in the Art Nouveau style.

has been with the firm for 60 years.

Art glass constituted about 75 percent of Schneider's production up to 1925; from 1925 to 1930, it represented only 40 percent of the factory's output. The manufacture of art glass became unprofitable and was soon discontinued. Schneider glass was distributed in the United States through importers; they did not maintain a showroom or shop of their own in America. The clear crystal ware currently produced by this firm is being distributed in France and other countries in Western Europe, as well as in Mexico, Japan, and Australia.

During the German occupation of World War II, the glassworks at Epinay-sur-Seine was used by the German army as a warehouse, and all literature and catalogs pertaining to the art glass products made by Schneider disappeared.

All of the glass made by this firm bears its signature—the name "Schneider" in script or block letters. The engraved signature in script was used prior to 1925; thereafter only the finest pieces of their glass were so marked. About 1925 or 1926, the name Schneider, in large, printed letters, was used; this signature was produced by roughing the glass with a jet of sand over a stencil.

The script signature can be found in four variations: "Schneider;" "Schneider" preceded by a representation of a vase; "Schneider, France"; and "Schneider, France" preceded by a representation of a vase.

Compote of mottled pink glass with amethyst-colored knop stem; wrought iron base decorated with orange-colored fruits mottled with blue.

The block letter signature has been found in only two variations: "Schneider"; and "Schneider, France."

The signature in script is sometimes filled in with gold or red, and possibly in other colors, too. The writer has pieces of Schneider glass with an additional engraved signature in script—"Ovington," or "Ovington, New York." These pieces were distributed by the firm of Ovington

Vase of mottled colors blown into a wrought iron framework—purple at base with orange spatter, shading into blue and purple, upper portion pale blue.

Brothers which operated an elegant retail china and glass establishment on Fifth Avenue in New York City, and a summer store at Bar Harbor, Maine.

Most collectors of art glass are familiar with the mottled glass made by Schneider. Generally these wares are found in the form of vases, bowls, compotes, pitchers, candleholders, wine glasses, etc., and in vivid colors —usually a combination of two or more colors. Various shades of red, orange, yellow, blue, green, purple, and brown were used. The beautiful effects which were obtained with the mixing of contrasting colors were said to have been inspired by the French Impressionists. The French called this mottled glass *Intercalaires*. Charles Schneider had a penchant for beautiful colors, but the one most frequently found today is an orange shade which was very popular about 1926. This color, which Schneider called "Tango," was one of the most difficult to produce.

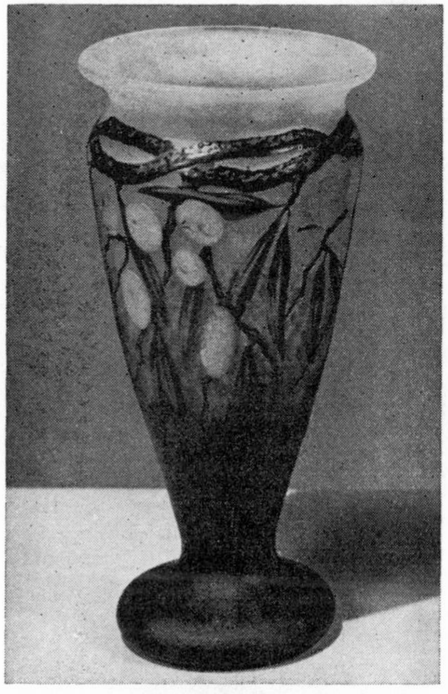

Another fine piece of the Art Nouveau style of Schneider's cameo glass.

The cloudy effect of Schneider's mottled glass is often called "Cluthra," but this is not correct as most of these wares have very few bubbles in the glass—a factor that is a prerequisite for the Cluthra wares made by Steuben and others. Some of the most interesting pieces of Schneider's mottled glass have applied glass feet, stems, handles, knobs, or some

LEFT: Pitcher of mottled red glass with splashes of blue; applied amethyst handle; height 14 inches.

other decorations in a different color than the body glass. At times these applied decorations are made of transparent colored glass, mottled, or cloudy glass.

Between 1924 and 1930, Charles Schneider often combined ironwork with his art glass productions. Compotes with wrought iron bases, and vases with an iron framework into which the plastic glass was blown, are among the items collectors can encounter. These represent some of the most interesting Schneider pieces.

Not all Schneider art glass is opaque or mottled. The writer's collection includes a tall amethyst vase with cut back geometric design; a transparent dark amber vase with splashes of red; a dark amber decanter of bubbly glass with an applied orange trim; a large vaseline-colored bowl; a French blue planter, quite bubbly, with clear applied handles; and a red-orange vase in crackle glass.

Charles Schneider also made many pieces of cameo glass, using both acid etching and hand cutting, and enamelled decoration. The writer also owns a flaming red opaque iridescent vase which very nearly approximates the rare Rouge Flambé color made by Frederick Carder at Steuben.

It is difficult to describe Schneider glass in a way that does justice to its beauty. Translucence is an important part of its charm, and it is most exciting when strong sunlight shines through it. The imagination of the artist was expressed in a variety of colors, shapes, and sizes. There seems never to have been any hesitation to experiment with unconventional combinations of color. Perhaps that explains why, though the glass was conceived in the Art Nouveau period, it fits so well in a contemporary setting.

Cut Glass of the Brilliant Period, 1880-1915

by HARRY W. HARTMAN

(1) Lamp in Chair Bottom and Hobstar pattern, triple mitre cutting; few lamps were made, and examples are relatively uncommon today. (2) Vase, made to order in 1900 at a reputed $400 would cost $700-1,000 to duplicate today, yet it sold within the last five years for $150; 26" high, 8" wide across top opening, glass itself ¾" thick. (3) Basket, 21" high, 15" across top at handle, glass itself almost ½" thick, etching of birds on flanges do not show in picture; baskets, stylish in the 1890s as centerpieces, are still popular, the large size in mint condition especially sought. Estimated replacement cost of this piece $300-400, 1955 sale price, $10..

CUT Glass of the Brilliant Period is perhaps the most generally maligned, misunderstood, and least appreciated of current collectibles. Because of the lateness of its manufacture, brides of 1910–1915, who even as their mothers, counted it by the dozens among their wedding gifts, are understandably loathe to admit it "antique"—or even collectible, nor do they encourage their children, the young marrieds of the '30's, to do so. Painfully conscious of the quantities they have given away, sold at rummage, or otherwise disposed of as "too heavy to use," "too cumbersome to store," or just plain "too old fashioned," they decry its worth.

Forward looking collectors, on the other hand, fascinated by its innate elegance and exquisite workmanship, and aware that such cutting will never again be done for any widespread distribution, have for the past ten years or so been quietly picking up the beautiful pieces characteristic of the 1880s and 1890s. They feel that as an art form, Cut Glass is as important of preservation as Webb's Cameo or Tiffany Favrille of the same era.

Such strong personal bias, coupled with the tendency of the uninformed to class all cut glass alike, has led to a wide disparity in the prices asked for cut glass pieces, even in neighboring shops. Many a canny collector who knows and favors earlier types of cut glass will pass up fine pieces of the Brilliant Period as "too late" —and many a dealer of the same persuasion will let unusual pieces pass through his hands at a fraction of their worth. Others, equally unknowing, yet fearing to miss a trick, will put premium prices on glass which is actually only an imitation of true cut pieces. To the knowledgable buyer, the glass itself, the cutting, brilliance, shape, maker, marks and patterns are all important factors in determining the worth of the piece.

Twenty years ago few dealers stocked cut glass. Those who did would dare ask no more than a few dollars for even exceptional pieces. Today it is not unusual to see good pieces retail from $50 to $100 or even higher. Predicated on the price increases of Victorian Art Glass in the past ten years, cut glass may be expected to soar to unprecedented high figures within a very few years. Dealers, casual collectors and "hoarders," who have hitherto been completely disinterested, should shake off their apathy and learn to recognize this elegant and beautifully executed glass for what it is—and will be.

Below is given a short short story on the whys and hows and whats of cut glass of the Brilliant Period. The illustrations and their captions tell the tale of the economic advantages of recognizing and buying fine pieces of this truly beautiful glass.

What

Glass decorated with an incisory ornamentation by application to a moving wheel, has, since earliest times, been known as "cut." The geometrical lines of its designs which form prisms or facets distinguish it from other ornamental forms.

When

Cut Glass was known to the Assyrians in 722 B. C., to the Persians in 532 B. C., in Ancient Rome. It was old in Constantinople by 1451, and new in Italy in the 14th century. It was "rediscovered" in Germany at the end of the 16th century under Rudolph II, who brought rock crystal cutters from Milan to take charge of the crystal and glass cutting works he established at Prague. A hundred years later, England had developed the art and was exporting cut glass to the Continent. In America, the Early Period of cut glass began at Baron Steigel's manufactory in Manheim, Pennsylvania, in 1771, and lasted until 1830. The Middle Period, determined by a high tariff that shut out importations, marked the beginnings of domestic styles and designs—simplicity was the keynote—and extended from 1830 to 1880. Technical advances in glassmaking which made possible a crystal clear glass, heavy enough for the cutting of deep and intricate designs, issued in the Brilliant Period in 1880.

How

Cut Glass was always a symbol of wealth and elegance. Though the new glassmaking techniques of the Brilliant Period provided for quantity production and the general prosperity of the country made it available to almost everybody, it never lost its luxury appeal. It was never cheap. Elegant and desired, it proved the ideal gift for weddings, anniversaries, and other occasions-to-be-remembered in the 1880s and 1890s.

The expense in producing cut glass lay in the skilled handwork involved. First the designer outlined the pattern on lead glass blanks which had either been blown off hand or in a paste mold. Then the rougher, using steel wheels with mitred edges and with a trickling sand and water abrasive, made the first deep incisions. The smoother refined these first incisions and cut the smaller more intricate portions of the design, and with stone wheels smoothed the roughly cut surfaces. Polishers worked with wooden wheels and a pumice and water abrasive to produce a lustrous appearance and remove imperfections, and finally with rapidly revolving brushes and putty powder (tin oxide) to give a high finish. The men who performed these four operations were all highly skilled—and highly paid.

Between 1895 and 1900, economy measures were being sought. The substitution of a hydrochloric acid bath for the polishing processes allowed one or two men to polish the output of a large factory, work that previously might have entailed as many as 40 skilled workers.

Alas, Economy

Having tested the benefits of economy without any appreciable loss of prestige to their product, manufacturers began to look for other means to cheapen production. They found in

Owen's invention of the fire finished pressed blank a way to cut down on the hand labor of the rougher and smoother, and to do away with the hitherto unavoidable loss of metal in the first cutting. By the use of this fire pressed blank, which came to the workmen already pressed with the first deep incisions, pieces of the same shape, patterns and weight could be produced much more cheaply and rapidly.

But the economy proved costly, for in the pressing process, the refractory surface was destroyed and the essential prismatic brilliance and the sharp cutting of true cut glass was lost. With this "imitation," the manufacturers had unwittingly sounded the knell for true cut glass. Discriminating collectors today repudiate glass cut on fire pressed blanks just as the discriminating did when it first appeared. When these pressed blanks were used, slight ridges will be found on the inside of the piece opposite the deeper incisions on the outside. The glass, too, is frequently, but not always, inferior.

Engraved and Etched

Engraved glass, which is decorated by moving copper wheels, usually with a linseed oil and pumice abrasive, requires even more time and skill than cutting. Most engravings were left unpolished to produce a greyish contrast to the pure crystal. Etched glass is not cut, but produced by the application of a corroding acid. Both engraving and etching are to be found in combination with cutting on various pieces.

Makers

Among the many well known glasshouses producing finest quality cut glass during the Brilliant Period were Dorflinger and Sons, H. C. Fry Glass Company, Gillander and Sons, T. G. Hawkes Glass Company, Libbey Glass Company, the Pairpoint Corporation and the Phoenix Glass Company. A great many cutting shops, some of them short-lived, bought their glass blanks from large glass manufactories and engaged their own designers and cutters, often turning out exceptional pieces. The Corning Glass Company which had no cutting shop of its own supplied many such firms. One of these, J. Hoare & Company of Corning, New York, became one of the largest glass cutting shops in the world. The Pairpoint Corporation in New Bedford is known to have furnished blanks for several shops, as did almost all the large glass companies. Frequently the quality of the glass in unidentified pieces is such that the experienced collector will associate it at sight with the glasshouse which supplied the blank.

Trademarks

Between 1895 and 1905 many trade-

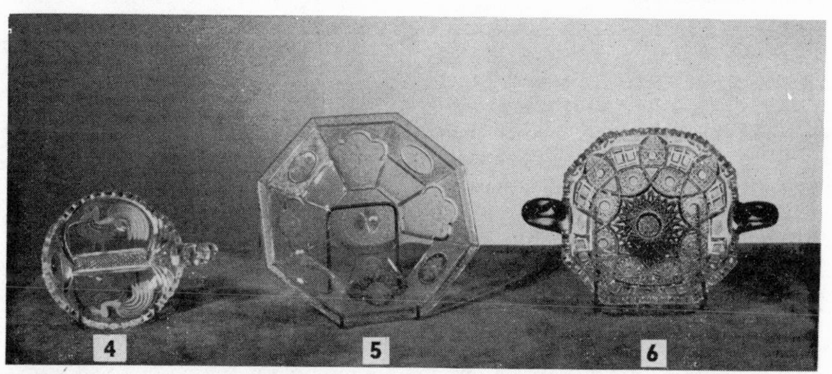

(4) Nappy showing use of both cutter's and engraver's wheel to achieve striking effect; etched rooster motif is unusual. (5) Very heavy octagonal platter with relatively narrow edges increasing to ½" thickness in center; etched flower and basket motifs; marked with acid etched "S" in wreath suggesting Sinclaire, who produced fine cut glass on Corning blanks; though of finest quality triple mitre cutting and superb engraving characteristic of top grade American manufacturer, it was sold at a N. Y. Antiques Show as "a fine piece of French glass" for $12. (6) Extremely rare piece with blue center and handles, rest of glass clear.

marks were registered. Some, printed on paper stickers, were affixed to the piece with glue; others were etched in acid on each piece. The latter alone can furnish infallible identification. While marked pieces are definitely sought, many outstanding and unusually beautiful pieces are to be found with no identification and should not be discounted because they bear no signature.

Hawkes

Several of the examples pictured here were made by Hawkes, readily identified by his simple "H" or his two hawks in a shamrock mark. All of his pieces after 1895 were presumably trademarked, and he used no pressed blanks. Thomas G. Hawkes, a descendant of five generations of glassmakers and cutters in England and Ireland, came to Brooklyn, New York, in 1863, to set up a cutting shop. In 1880, he moved to Corning, New York, cutting fine glass on blanks to his own specifications by the Corning Glass Company. Later, with his son, Samuel, and Frederick Carder of Stourbridge, England, he established the Steuben Glass Company in Corning for the manufacture of his own glass. Pieces made by Hawkes at this factory from 1903 bear the acid etched "Steuben." His Steuben Company was sold to the Corning Class Company in 1918 and is now a subsidiary of that company.

Of special note is the signed Hawkes pieces (Fig. 19) which bears in addition to the usual trademark the acid etched "Gravic Glass." This refers to a steel cutting technique used to create a greyish flower design, usually iris or asters. Due to the expense involved, only a limited number of these pieces were made, all about 1900. These are rare, and a piece with the "Gravic Glass" mark is a once-in-a-lifetime find.

Fry

Henry Clay Fry is another who marked much of his glass, using an acid etched "Fry" in a shield as his trademark. His glass was of exceptional brilliance, but it is the unusual shapes of his handmade blanks which made his work distinctive. His factory at Rochester, Pennsylvania, continued in production until 1929.

It was Fry who, as president of the National Glass combine, a syndicate of ten glass companies organized in 1899, bought the invention for pressed glass blanks, and unwittingly hastened the end of the cut glass industry in America.

Patterns

The patterns of Brilliant Period cut glass are many. They include the familiar motives of curved split, chair bottom, hob-star, and notched prism, as well as earlier hobnail, block, fan and strawberry diamond patterns. While a great many patterns were patented by the glasshouses where they originated, they were continuously being copied and adapted. When the United States Glass Company was organized in 1892 as a holding company for seventeen affiliated companies, the identity of many patterns was lost in volume production. This holding company was economy minded. All short cuts to production, including pressed blanks, were used. However, for collectors seeking a complete table setting, a United States Company pattern, produced in quantity, offers the best opportunity for a successful search.

LIBBEY'S MODERN AMERICAN SERIES

Glass with Class

by WILLIAM AND IDA LUTTRELL

All pieces, signed Libbey, from the authors' collection photographed by W. T. Hall.

IN THE late 1930s, as the depression eased its grip on the United States, Americans were ready to put the past behind them. It was a time for looking to the future; a time for seeking styles of tomorrow in everything from music to the decorative arts. The Libbey Glass Company reflected this trend in taste with the production of a line of glass called the "Modern American Series."

The person responsible for creating this fine glass was Edwin W. Fuerst. He was hired as director of design by Owens-Illinois in 1930 prior to their acquisition of the Libbey Glass Company, an establishment with a rich history of glass production in America.

The Libbey Glass Company, the oldest glass company in continuous production in the United States, is a

Spiral optic rose bowl. Clear blown crystal. Height: 7 inches.

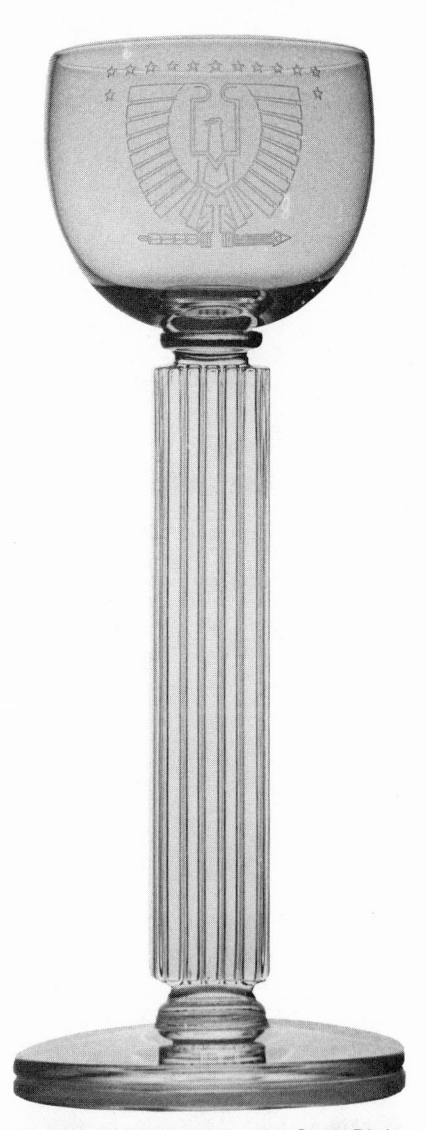

Wine glass designed for the State Dining Room of the Federal Building at the 1939 New York World's Fair. Plate etched crystal bowl attached to ribbed rectangular stem. Later produced without the eagle and stars and called the Embassy pattern. Height: 6 3/4 inches.

descendant of the New England Glass Company which was established in 1818. After the New England Glass Company moved to Toledo, Ohio, in 1889, it adopted the name of its owner, Edward Drummond Libbey. The company continued to operate under that name, even after it was acquired by Owens-Illinois in 1936.

The "Modern American Series" that Mr. Fuerst designed was created by Libbey craftsmen, who were the best available. This clear, blown lead crystal with its simple lines was a stark contrast to the ornate forms of glass of the Victorian era and the colorful glass produced during the Art Nouveau period. This series encompassed a variety of patterns from the flowing design of the spiral optic to the rectilinear lines of the *Embassy* pattern. The use of heavy thick glass in some of the vases offers a hint of Art Deco, while the square block foot of the *Knickerbocker* pattern and the rectangular stems of the *Embassy* pattern are more obvious examples of that style. Only occasional pieces in this series are decorated by limited copper wheel cutting. The goal of the artist and craftsmen in producing this glass was to create a crystal of such flaw-

Monticello wine glass. Blown crystal attached to ribbed columnar stem. According to the Libbey catalog, "As American in feeling as Monticello's columns." Height: 7 inches.

Bubble stem compote. The trapped air bubbles "appear to rise from the clear base merging into the bubble-like bowl above," according to the Libbey catalog. Height: 5 inches.

less brilliance that the quality of the glass itself would be dominant over the design. Therefore it did not require color or cutting to enhance it. In striving to make the finest glass possible one hundred melts were compounded before a suitable formula was developed to produce this glass and its quality cannot be denied.

The previously mentioned *Embassy* pattern has the most colorful history of any of the patterns in this series. It came into being as a result of the Libbey Glass Company having been chosen to produce the glassware used in the State Dining Room of the Federal Building at the 1939 New York World's Fair. The theme of this fair was "The Worlds of Tomorrow" and the design of the glassware was coordinated with the other items designated for the State Dining Room. A clear, blown crystal bowl attached to a ribbed rectangular stem with a clear circular foot constituted the shape of this unique stemware. The bowl is decorated with a stylized eagle flanked by 13 stars representing the original States. Edwin Fuerst was the ori-

Heavy blown crystal vase. Also pictured in the Libbey catalog engraved with a stallion's head. Height: 6 3/4 inches.

Cordial decanter set. Reminiscent of Art Deco, clear blown decanter attached to block base. Eight cordial glasses completed the set. Height of decanter including stopper: 11 inches. Height of cordial: 2 1/4 inches.

ginator of this pattern while Walter Dorwin Teague, designer of the building that housed that State Dining Room, created the plate etched decoration. An unusual feature of this pattern is that all the stems from the cordial to the goblet, except for a 5-1/2 inch parfait, were of equal dimensions and height. The King and Queen of England were the first to use this crystalware at a luncheon given in their honor at the State Dining Room which afforded the Libbey Company much prestigious publicity. At the close of the World's Fair the remainder of this glassware was shipped to the White House where it was used on State occasions as late as the 1950s. Because of its favorable reception this glassware, without the eagle and stars, was included in the "Modern American Series" and called the *Embassy* pattern. Since none of the crested pieces were made for sale they are considered extremely rare. While the non-crested pieces are not plentiful they are more readily available to the collector.

According to the price list published in the 1941 Libbey catalog there are six other patterns of crystal table service in the "Modern American Series." Although these patterns lack the glamorous background of the *Embassy* pattern they are equal in quality and appeal. Pictured in the catalog are the *Concord, Knickerbocker, American Prestige, Waterford, Monticello,* and *Hermitage* patterns.

Two of these patterns, the *Knickerbocker,* which was characterized by a square block crystal foot attached to a clear thin crystal bowl, and the *Hermitage,* highlighted by unusual block cutting at the base of the tumblers and footed cocktail, were carried over from the 1933 Libbey-Nash production line. Perhaps the similarity of style prompted the Libbey Company to include them in the "Modern American Series."

Identifiable features in the other patterns include the four-sided stem attached to a terraced foot of the *American Prestige* pattern, heavy crystal bowl joined to a single knop stem of the *Waterford* pattern and the heavy fluted round base of the *Concord* pattern. Elegant simplicity is expressed in the *Monticello* pattern, consisting of stemware formed by joining a bell-shaped blown bowl to a ribbed cylindrical column. The Libbey catalog had this to say about the *Monticello* pattern: "The master

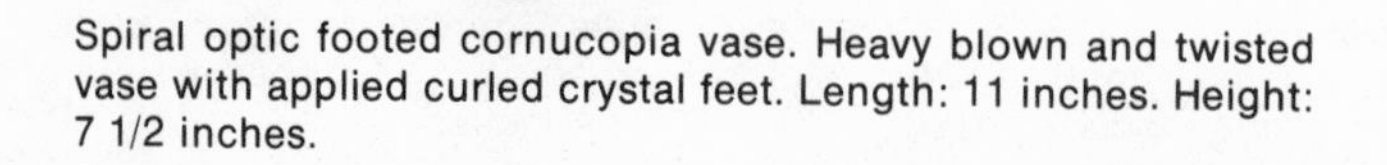

Spiral optic footed cornucopia vase. Heavy blown and twisted vase with applied curled crystal feet. Length: 11 inches. Height: 7 1/2 inches.

designer, Thomas Jefferson would have liked this stately pattern, as American in feeling as Monticello's columns." Some of these patterns were available in complete table settings, others were limited in variety to five pieces.

While thin, fragile glass was used in the tableware, the decorative pieces were fashioned from thick, heavy glass with a clarity and brillance reminiscent of the Steuben glass produced today. A wide selection of forms is pictured in the Libbey catalog including vases, rose bowls, compotes, candlesticks, decanters, bowls, and candy jars. Two types of cornucopias were made, one of plain blown crystal which rests vertically on a polished square foot, and the other which was blown, pulled and twisted into a spiral optic effect and supported by two curled crystal feet. Because of their durability, the decorative pieces have survived handsomely and can be found by the collector with a diligent eye. More rare are those pieces embellished by copper wheel engraving. Among these are various shaped vases decorated with animals such as herons, giraffes, ducks, and gazelles, a footed vase engraved with a fleur de lis, and a covered candy dish ornamented by a leaping fawn. All the glass in this series is signed with an acid etched full Libbey signature.

In addition to people who are attracted to it for its own merit, this glass appeals to three types of collectors; those seeking World's Fair memorabilia, Libbey glass collectors, and persons interested in Art Deco. It can be found for sale in antique shops, at antique shows and advertised in magazines and journals specializing in collectibles. Examples of Libbey's "Modern American Series" of glassware can be seen in the Toledo Museum of Fine Arts, Toledo, Ohio. It is also housed in private collections such as that of an Art Deco collector in Houston, Texas, who displays his set of Embassy stemware in a zebrawood cabinet.

This glass, which had its beginning on the heels of the depression, was terminated by the advent of World War II. When the United States entered the war, the Libbey Glass Company turned to the production of articles essential to the war effort and the Modern American Series of glassware was discontinued. It spelled the end of production of fine handcrafted crystal by the Libbey Glass Company.

Although the period of production was brief and not a great quantity of the "Modern American Series" was produced, there are pieces available for the collector today.

Cornucopia vase. Block crystal base supports clear blown vase. Height: 8 inches.

The Fostoria Glass Company's Fancy Glass Lighting

by ALBERT CHRISTIAN REVI

No. 1 Candelabra, three light, with optional flower vase. No height given in the catalog.

No. 3 Banquet Candelabra, seven light, with "U drop prisms." Height 30 inches; spread 19 inches.

No. 7 Candelabra with arms of twisted glass was made in 3, 4, 5 or 6 lights, with either a flower vase or candle holder in center. Height as shown in the catalog 23 inches; spread 15 inches; base diameter 7 inches.

THE Fostoria Glass Company is one of a very few surviving manufacturers of fancy pressed glass established in the late 19th century. Originally located in Fostoria, Ohio, in 1887, it moved to its present location in Moundsville, West Virginia, in 1891. An abundant supply of natural gas and coal needed to operate their furnaces was their reason for making this move.

While Fostoria's pressed glass patterns are well-known to collectors,

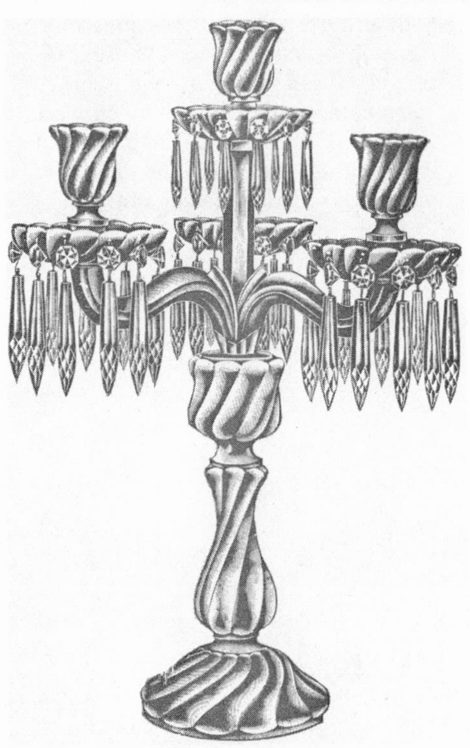

No. 2 Candelabra, four lights, with "U drop prisms." Height 21 inches; spread 12 inches.

No. 13 five light Candelabra was also made in 4, 6 and 7 lights. Came with or without prisms.

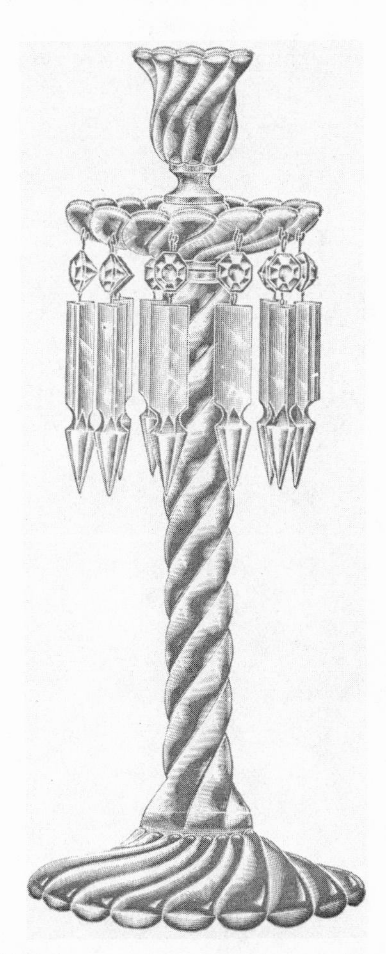

1103 Lustre with "Spearhead Prisms" was produced in 14½, 18½, and 22½ inch heights.

their fancy candlesticks, candelabras and oil lamps are not. Often these beautifully fashioned lighting devices are mistaken for similar wares made by the Baccarat glassworks in France. While they are very near look-alikes, there are some distinctive design features, as shown in our illustrations, which make them recognizable to collectors as Fostoria productions.

Single candlesticks and candelabras with two or more candle sockets were produced in a twisted rope design; many of them were hung with prisms to enhance their appearance and heighten their reflective values.

No. 3 Banquet Candelabra, four light, with "U drop prisms." Height 28 inches; spread 12 inches.

Still others resemble European designs of the same period. Those illustrated here appeared in Fostoria's 1904 catalog. Since no colors were indicated in their descriptions of these wares we can assume they were produced only in clear crystal.

Left: "Diana Princess" oil lamp; height 21 inches. **Right:** "Colonial Princess oil lamp; height 20 inches.